PARABLES
of
Redemption

PARABLES
of
Redemption

The Restored Doctrine of the Atonement as Taught
in the Parables of Jesus Christ

C. Robert Line
Ronald E. Bartholomew
R. Scott Burton
Robert England Lee
Craig Frogley
Andrew C. Skinner

Horizon Publishers
Springville, Utah

ISBN 13: 978-0-88290-834-2

Published by Horizon Publishers, an imprint of Cedar Fort, Inc., 2373 W. 700 S., Springville, UT, 84663
Distributed by Cedar Fort, Inc., www.cedarfort.com

LIBRARY OF CONGRESS CATALOGING-IN-PUBLICATION DATA

Parables of redemption : the restored doctrine of the atonement as taught in
the parables of Jesus Christ / Craig R. Frogley ... [et al.].
   p. cm.
 ISBN-13: 978-0-88290-834-2 (alk. paper)
  1. Atonement—Church of Jesus Christ of Latter-day Saints. 2. Atonement—Mormon Church.
3. Jesus Christ—Mormon interpretations. 4. Jesus Christ—Parables 5. Church of Jesus Christ
of Latter-day Saints—Doctrines. 6. Mormon Church—Doctrines. I. Frogley, Craig R.
  BX8643.A85P37 2007
  226.8'06—dc22
                          2007030508

Cover design by Nicole Williams
Cover design © 2007 by Lyle Mortimer
Edited by Annaliese B. Cox
Typeset by Kimiko M. Hammari

Printed in the United States of America

10 9 8 7 6 5 4 3 2 1

Printed on acid-free paper

PREFACE

Many, many books have been published on the parables of the New Testament. Does the world need another one? Do the Latter-day Saints? Probably not—unless you are talking about this one. Compiler C. Robert "Rob" Line and his fellow authors have conceived a unique volume, an in-depth examination of specific parables of the Master that teach us directly about the Atonement of Jesus Christ, that illuminate aspects of his unique act of redemption, and that help us better understand the mercy, justice, depth, and power of his infinite sacrifice for all humankind. There are examinations of New Testament parables that touch on this theme but none that focus our attention wholly on this, the centerpiece of the plan of redemption.

If the Atonement of Jesus Christ is the most important event in time or all eternity (it is!), and if "all things which have been given of God from the beginning of the world, unto man, are the typifying of [Christ]" (2 Nephi 11:4) (they are!), then it is only natural that specific parables presented by the very Anointed One himself would have as part of their profound message the Atonement of the Anointed One (they do!). This is a stunning realization—and well it should be. For we are able to read and experience not only other testimonies and confirmations of the incomparable redemption provided to us by our Lord, but also understand the truth that Jesus used every teaching opportunity, every teaching tool and technique, to point disciples and potential disciples to the workings of the Atonement in their lives. The parables of redemption help all audiences, ancient and modern, to understand more completely how and where the Atonement fits into the Father's plan for his children.

Great teachers in almost every religious tradition have used figures of speech and illustrative stories (allegories, fables, parables, and the like) to present their messages. This is especially true of the towering figures in Jewish tradition, the master teachers of ancient Israel who we know as the rabbis. The word *rabbi* comes from a Hebrew root meaning "great" and literally means "my great one" or, by extension, "my master" or "my teacher." The rabbis were masters precisely because they had mastered their subject and taught their disciples in a masterly manner—by spoken illustration and metaphor as well as personal example.

The Master of masters, Jesus of Nazareth, was, in part, a product of his time and culture. He drew upon images and cultural mores also found in the teachings of his rabbinic contemporaries. He taught like them and was himself called Rabbi by even the acknowledged political and religious rulers of the Jewish people (see John 3:2).

Thus, we do not diminish the stature of Jesus when we frankly admit that he adopted well-known parables or elements of them and recast them to suit his own eternal purposes. In fact, therein lies the tale, for Jesus' purposes were far different from those of the rabbis. Under Jesus' transforming touch, parables became the most profound expressions of eternal truth, namely that repentance, redemption, and resurrection come to all humankind only through his atoning sacrifice, and recognition of that sacrifice must occupy a central place in one's mind and heart in order to realize the goal of eternal life.

The parables of redemption demonstrate the same reasons Jesus used parables during his ministry of instruction as we see demonstrated in the other parables he presented:

1. Parables were part of the world in which Jesus grew up and lived as an adult. The greatest teachers and rabbis of Jesus' era used parables. It could be that Jesus used both the general outline as well as specific elements of parables taught by others precisely because they were so well known and his listeners already recognized the stock-in-trade stories he presented. With Jesus' parables, however, there was not only a new, singular application, but as with all his teachings, "he taught them as one having authority, and not as the scribes" (Matthew 7:29). Perhaps people "were astonished at his doctrine" (Matthew 7:28) because, though they recognized certain elements, his parables had a unique tone and application.

2. Parables teach by analogies that are not easily forgotten. The Greek word *parabole,* from which our English word *parable* derives, means "to set side by side or to compare one thing to another." It is

the equivalent of the Hebrew *mashal*. Because parables compared or set principles of the gospel side by side with ordinary objects, common events, or familiar circumstances of life, they could be readily identified, understood, and remembered. Each parable was drawn from life; each was a short story that encompassed a spiritual message. By placing real-life stories familiar to all people side by side with gospel principles, the Savior could stimulate his hearers' thinking, illustrate a point, and give ordinary, easily visualized reminders of the eternal principles he taught.

3. Parables have a double use in communicating messages—they can simultaneously veil or unveil concepts, reveal or conceal meaning, according to an individual's spiritual capacity and ability to receive. Thus, the Savior could simultaneously teach truths to those ready to receive them and hide meaning from the unprepared. The Savior explained to his disciples, "Therefore speak I to them in parables: because they seeing see not; and hearing they hear not, neither do they understand" (Matthew 13:13). Every person could be taught a different but true lesson depending on each one's understanding of the objects used in the parable. According to the Bible dictionary, "The parable conveys to the hearer religious truth exactly in proportion to his faith and intelligence; to the dull and unintelligent it is a mere story, 'seeing they see not,' while to the instructed and spiritual it reveals the mysteries or secrets of the kingdom of heaven. Thus it is that the parable exhibits the condition of all true knowledge. Only he who seeks finds."[1] To "learn" gospel truths we must pay a price. The gifts of the spirit and an unshakable testimony of the gospel are not unearned blessings.

4. By teaching in parables, the Lord protects unprepared individuals from more truth than they can live—a merciful way in which to teach. Exposure to the unadulterated truth as Jesus was capable of teaching it would have put listeners in an untenable position—requiring them to live principles beyond their capability to live, thus interfering with their agency.

5. On occasion the Savior taught in parables so that his listeners could not misunderstand his intention. At one point he said, "I speak in parables; that your unrighteousness may be rewarded

unto you" (JS—M 21:34). This is specifically true of the Jewish leaders of Jesus' day, some of whom were responsible for his death. They were condemned because they understood but refused to act accordingly: "Woe unto you, scribes and Pharisees, hypocrites! for ye are like unto whited sepulchres, which indeed appear beautiful outward, but are within full of dead men's bones, and of all uncleanness. Even so ye also outwardly appear righteous unto men, but within ye are full of hypocrisy and iniquity" (Matthew 23:27–28).

It is especially true for the parables of redemption to say that the spiritual condition of one's mind and heart made it possible for contemporary listeners to apply the lessons taught and internalize the intended meanings of those parables. I believe that many, if not most, of the Jewish leaders and educated listeners living in Jesus' day understood what Jesus meant. After all, they lived their daily lives in the world of rabbinic metaphor and meaning. And they saw before their very eyes the real life stories and cultural elements on which the parables were based (whereas we in modern times do not). But, they did not apply or internalize the teachings of these parables due to pride, laziness, stubbornness, or hypocrisy. How unfortunate.

In our day, we may count ourselves fortunate that the compiler and individual authors of this little but significant volume have given us an important gift by explicitly connecting the doctrine of the Atonement to specific parables Jesus taught. I believe this collection of essays is a welcome addition to the literature on parables. More important, however, it helps us understand a little better that event which is the center of eternity—the Atonement of Jesus Christ.

—*Andrew C. Skinner*
Executive Director of the Neal A. Maxwell Institute for
Religious Scholarship, Brigham Young University

Notes
1. Bible Dictionary, "parable," 740–41.

Contents

The Savior's Grace Is Sufficient

Understanding the Parable of the Laborers in the Vineyard

by C. Robert Line

Several years ago I had an intriguing conversation with a good friend regarding the parable of the laborers in the vineyard. This individual was a well-respected leader in the community and very conversant with the restored gospel. He was a hardworking, no-nonsense type who was basically a self-made man with a somewhat austere and confident character. To his credit, he really tried the best he could to live all facets of the gospel with exactness; indeed, I have never encountered his equal.

We happened to be talking one day about the gospel and associated symbolism that we sometimes encounter in the scriptures and in the temples. The topic of parables came up. It just so happened at the time of this conversation I had just finished a semester of teaching an institute of religion course entitled The Parables of Jesus, so naturally I was excited to discuss the topic with him. Out of the blue he asked, "What is your favorite parable?" That was an easy answer. Although there are many parables that I love, the one that, for me at least, has been the most stimulating and the most rewarding to study is the parable of the laborers in the vineyard.

Upon telling him this, his countenance literally dropped, and a look of consternation came over him—it was as if I had just committed some horrible crime. Although he was a friend, and a close one at that, you would have never known it at that moment. He gazed at me with a piercing stare and simply exclaimed, "You have got to be kidding me! Are you serious?"

To which I replied, "I am serious—it is my favorite parable."

His reply: "I hate that parable!"

I could really tell that he was sincere with his feelings and that he meant what he said. I asked him why he did not like the parable. With a tone of repugnance he declared, "It's just not fair!"

The Parable
Matthew 20:1–16

1 For the kingdom of heaven is like unto a man that is an householder, which went out early in the morning to hire labourers into his vineyard.

2 And when he had agreed with the labourers for a penny a day, he sent them into his vineyard.

3 And he went out about the third hour, and saw others standing idle in the marketplace,

4 And said unto them; Go ye also into the vineyard, and whatsoever is right I will give you. And they went their way.

5 Again he went out about the sixth and ninth hour, and did likewise.

6 And about the eleventh hour he went out, and found others standing idle, and saith unto them, Why stand ye here all the day idle?

7 They say unto him, Because no man hath hired us. He saith unto them, Go ye also into the vineyard; and whatsoever is right, that shall ye receive.

8 So when even was come, the lord of the vineyard saith unto his steward, Call the labourers, and give them their hire, beginning from the last unto the first.

9 And when they came that were hired about the eleventh hour, they received every man a penny.

10 But when the first came, they supposed that they should have received more; and they likewise received every man a penny.

11 And when they had received it, they murmured against the goodman of the house,

12 Saying, These last have wrought but one hour, and thou hast made them equal unto us, which have borne the burden and heat of the day.

13 But he answered one of them, and said, Friend, I do thee no wrong: didst not thou agree with me for a penny?

14 Take that thine is, and go thy way: I will give unto this last, even as unto thee.

15 Is it not lawful for me to do what I will with mine own? Is thine eye evil, because I am good?

16 So the last shall be first, and the first last: for many be called, but few chosen.

I have thought about the possible reasons my good friend, or anyone else for that matter, would react so negatively to this parable, and I have concluded that they probably do not understand the symbolic nature of parables.

The Purpose of Parables

Unlike most stories, which are simply that—stories, the Savior used parables to teach in-depth matters regarding himself, his gospel, and more important, his atoning sacrifice for mankind. These matters were so light-intensive that he had to exercise caution in teaching. The Savior was once asked by his disciples why he taught in parables. His reply is instructive:

Matthew 13:11–13

11 It is given unto you to know the mysteries of the kingdom of heaven, but to them it is not given.

12 For whosoever hath, to him shall be given, and he shall have more abundance: but whosoever hath not, from him shall be taken away even that he hath.

13 Therefore speak I to them in parables: because they seeing see not; and hearing they hear not, neither do they understand.

Bruce R. McConkie explained it this way:

Our Lord used *parables* on frequent occasions during his ministry to teach gospel truths. His purpose, however, in telling these short stories was *not* to present the truths of his gospel in plainness so that all his hearers would understand. Rather it was so to phrase and hide the doctrine involved that only the spiritually literate would understand it, while those whose understandings were darkened would remain in darkness. . . . It is never proper to teach any person more than his spiritual capacity qualifies him to assimilate.[1]

The parable of the laborers in the vineyard is indeed a simple story, but there is much doctrine that lies beneath the surface. Those who see this parable as only a story about coins and investments might be prone to derive an interpretation based solely on a monetary mind-set. When seen this way, the parable is indeed unfair. But this is not about economics. This parable is about the Lord Jesus Christ and his gospel.

Interpreting Parables

It can be difficult at times to figure out the true meaning of a parable. Joseph Smith once gave a key to correct interpretation: "What is the rule of interpretation? Just no interpretation at all. Understand it precisely as it reads. I have a key by which I understand the scriptures. I enquire, what was the question which drew out the answer, or caused Jesus to utter the parable? . . . To ascertain its meaning, we must dig up the root and ascertain what it was that drew the saying out of Jesus."[2] Most parables are easier to understand once their context is understood. In the case of this parable, the context includes chapter 19, the chapter that precedes the parable.

Matthew 19:16–30

16 And, behold, one came and said unto him, Good Master, what good thing shall I do, that I may have eternal life?

17 And he said unto him, Why callest thou me good? there is none good but one, that is, God: but if thou wilt enter into life, keep the commandments.

18 He saith unto him, Which? Jesus said, Thou shalt do no murder, Thou shalt not commit adultery, Thou shalt not steal, Thou shalt not bear false witness,

19 Honour thy father and thy mother: and, Thou shalt love thy neighbour as thyself.

20 The young man saith unto him, All these things have I kept from my youth up: what lack I yet?

21 Jesus said unto him, If thou wilt be perfect, go and sell that thou hast, and give to the poor, and thou shalt have treasure in heaven: and come and follow me.

22 But when the young man heard that saying, he went away sorrowful: for he had great possessions.

23 Then said Jesus unto his disciples, Verily I say unto you, That a rich man shall hardly enter into the kingdom of heaven.

24 And again I say unto you, It is easier for a camel to go through the eye of a needle, than for a rich man to enter into the kingdom of God.

25 When his disciples heard it, they were exceedingly amazed, saying, Who then can be saved?

26 But Jesus beheld them, and said unto them, With men this is impossible; but with God all things are possible.

27 Then answered Peter and said unto him, Behold, we have forsaken all, and followed thee; what shall we have therefore?

28 And Jesus said unto them, Verily I say unto you, That ye which have followed me, in the regeneration when the Son of man shall sit in the throne of his glory, ye also shall sit upon twelve thrones, judging the twelve tribes of Israel.

29 And every one that hath forsaken houses, or brethren, or sisters, or father, or mother, or wife, or children, or lands, for my name's sake, shall receive an hundredfold, and shall inherit everlasting life.

30 But many that are first shall be last; and the last shall be first.

These verses supply the context to understand the parable. It is interesting to note that Peter is the person whose response provides the impetus for the parable. Usually we think of the Savior directing his reprimands toward the Pharisees and Scribes—such is not the case in this instance. Elder McConkie explains:

> This difficult parable is closely linked with what goes before, and can only be understood in connection with it. It rebukes the spirit of Peter's enquiry, "We have left all and followed thee; what shall we have?" (Matt. 19:27). The Twelve through Peter had demanded a superlatively great reward, because they had been called first and had labored longest. Such a reward had been promised them, should they prove worthy of it (Matt. 19:28), though at the same time it was darkly hinted, that some outside the apostolic circle would prove in the end more worthy than some of the apostles.[3]

The irony of Peter's request is unmistakable—"We have given up everything, so what's in it for us?" The thought is almost comical! It could be said that the parable of the laborers in the vineyard is thus a parable not just rebuking Peter, but anyone, for that matter, with an overblown sense of entitlement. Still, there is more to this parable. The perplexing question that is raised with regard to the seeming inequality of the rewards given for the work accomplished still demands explanation.

The Righteousness of the Reward

It is interesting to note the way in which the Lord of the Vineyard characterizes the reward—he speaks of it as not only being "right" but even "lawful"—that is to say, the reward is fair and does not violate spiritual law—the law of justice, that is. My friend who I mentioned at the outset, I am quite sure, might resort to the notion that "mercy cannot rob justice." The fact that the reward is described as being "lawful" would thus mean that mercy is not compromising justice in any way. So then, in what ways is the reward "right" and "lawful"?

First of all, everyone agreed on this. Each laborer knew what they would get for the work that would be accomplished. This should be reason enough. But the real reason the reward is just (and here is where we get to the heart of the parable) is that this profound teaching deals with the very essence of the grace and mercy of the Savior's Atonement. Surely we can understand to some extent the complaint of those who labored longest in the vineyard if we see it through the perspective of capitalism. That is to say, we reap what we sow. Not only do the scriptures sustain this notion, but likewise many philosophies and fiscal sound bites: "we get what we work for," "waste not want not," "an honest day's wage," and so forth. But once again, the interpretation of this parable is not one that seeks to teach capitalism nor any aspect of economic endeavor. This parable is teaching us about the grace and mercy of Jesus Christ.

The Penny and Eternal Life

The reward for laboring in the vineyard is not a result of our efforts alone. The penny, which symbolizes eternal life, is something that none of us can earn. We are told in the scriptures that it is by grace we are saved, after all we can do (see 2 Nephi 25:23). We are to rely wholly, not partially, upon the merits of Christ (see 2 Nephi 31:19). In this light it is absolutely ridiculous to think that a certain amount of labor or works (personal righteousness) will satisfy for the total price of eternal life. In this regard Dallin H. Oaks once taught: "Man unquestionably has impressive powers and can bring to pass great things by tireless efforts and indomitable will. But after all our obedience and good works, we cannot be saved from the effect of our sins without the grace extended by the atonement of Jesus Christ."[4] Similarly, Elder McConkie observed:

> Suppose we have the scriptures, the gospel, the priesthood, the Church, the ordinances, the organization, even the keys of the king-dom—everything that now is, down to the last jot and tittle—and yet there is no atonement of Christ. What then? Can we be saved? Will all our good works save us? Will we be rewarded for all our righteous-ness?
>
> Most assuredly we will not. We are not saved by works alone, no matter how good; we are saved because God sent his Son to shed his blood in Gethsemane and on Calvary that all through him might ran-somed be. We are saved by the blood of Christ. . . .
>
> To paraphrase Abinadi: "Salvation doth not come by the Church alone; and were it not for the atonement, given by the grace of God as a free gift, all men must unavoidably perish, and this notwithstanding the Church and all that appertains to it."[5]

None of us will ever really "earn" or deserve the "penny"—that is, no mortal will ever merit eternal life by works alone.

Another thought—the response of the first group of laborers to the reward given is interesting and a bit perplexing. We "have borne the burden and heat of the day." When one contemplates the murmuring response of those who labored all day in the vineyard, especially in light of the interpretation, the expression is ironic at best and absolutely absurd at worst: "Oh, how difficult it has been to keep the commandments. Oh, how horrible it has been to be in the covenant relationship. Oh, the drudgery of having true happiness and peace my whole life. Oh, the burden of having the joy of the companionship of the Holy Ghost. I am so envious of those who have labored but one hour. I wish I could be like them . . . the darkness, the depression—oh, the exquisite misery I could have had during my life . . . the horrible pain of happiness!" One would expect that the lifetime enjoyment of peace and spiritual prosperity would be in and of itself its own reward, regardless of even greater rewards in the next life. Indeed the labor that we put forth, in the gospel at least, is more than just mere work—living the gospel is a way of life. It is a lifestyle that carries its own recompense. One should be delighted to be a laborer in the Lord's vineyard.

When we truly contemplate this antagonistic attitude toward a righteous life, we are almost inclined to ask if the dreary all-day-long laborer was truly converted in the first place. Was he just going through the motions? Was his service and commitment to the kingdom for reasons other than those approved by Father in Heaven? Perhaps there are those who labor in the vineyard with a chip on their shoulder, as if they are doing the heavens some great favor. It is as though commitment to the kingdom is, in their minds, inextricably linked to a life of oppression, frowns, and loathing due to the arduous walk of Christlike living. Harry Emerson Fosdick perceptively observed:

> Some Christians carry their religion on their backs. It is a packet of beliefs and practices which they must bear. At times it grows heavy and they would willingly lay it down, but that would mean a break with old traditions, so they shoulder it again. But real Christians do not carry their religion, their religion carries them. It is not weight; it is wings. It lifts them up, it sees them over hard places, it makes the universe seem friendly, life purposeful, hope real, sacrifice worthwhile. It sets them free from fear, futility, discouragement, and sin—the great enslavers of men's souls. You can know a real Christian, when you see him, by his buoyancy.[6]

The Idle Laborers

Considering the fact that the penny represents the celestial glory of eternal life, these murmuring types and their associated companions (who endure, complain, and despise the life of service) might be shocked to realize that they might not, in the end, even want the reward for which they labored so zealously. "Service is not something we endure on this earth so we can earn the right to live in the celestial kingdom," said President Marion G. Romney. "Service is the very fiber of which an exalted life in the celestial kingdom is made."[7]

Perhaps the focus and attention of these disgruntled laborers is unduly placed on the late-arriving laborers who seemingly slide into heaven with no effort. Two thoughts are worth noting in this regard. First, these late arriving types, who we are told stood idle in the marketplace, are not idle in the sense of being lazy, complacent, or even rebellious. When asked why they were idle these workers responded by saying, "Because no man hath hired us." It is apparent from this phrase that these workers were in the marketplace, wanted to be hired, and were willing to work—but none was available at the time. Nevertheless they waited; diligently, patiently, they waited for work—no matter how much or how little. They did not go home or to the pool hall to pass the time.

Surely these types should be credited for enduring the uncertainty of unemployment and for displaying unwavering vigilance. Surely their long working counterparts should respect them for their fortitude, and even be grateful in the first place that they were afforded the blessed opportunity to be employed all day long. Anyone with experience in real living knows the horrible monotony and depressing curse of not being "anxiously engaged in a good cause" (D&C 58:27). Work is not drudgery; the lack thereof might be. "If you are poor, work. . . . If you are happy, work. Idleness gives room for doubts and fears. If disappointments come, keep right on working. If sorrow overwhelms you, . . . work. . . . When faith falters and reason fails, just work. When dreams are shattered and hope seems dead, work. Work as if your life were in peril. It really is. No matter what ails you, work. Work faithfully. . . . Work is the greatest remedy available for both mental and physical afflictions."[8]

Indeed, we would think that the first group of laborers would be grateful for the privileged to work. What a privilege to be an all-day laborer in the Lord's vineyard. What a privilege to have the light of the gospel constantly in our lives. Elder Packer once made an interesting observation regarding seemingly mundane moments in our life that, when seen through the proper perspective, are actually rewarding reveries of spiritual nourishment:

> Before entering the temple to begin the ordinance work, the companies frequently will assemble in the chapel in the annex portion of the building. Here the members wait until the full company is assembled. *Generally in life we would become impatient with waiting. To be first in a room and then be compelled to wait for the last to enter before proceeding would in other circumstances cause irritation.* In the temple it is just the opposite. *That waiting is regarded as a choice opportunity.* What a privilege it is to sit quietly without conversation and direct the mind to reverent and spiritual thoughts! It is a refreshment to the soul.[9]

So it is with being a laborer in the vineyard for the whole day—it is not and should not be an irritation that we are compelled to go through. It can and should be regarded as a choice opportunity!

Furthermore, we would expect that the long-laboring workers would look with compassion on those who truly wanted to work but were genuinely unable. In this regard it is worth noting that God can reward this last group equally with the first because of their willingness alone. We often misunderstand or completely ignore this aspect of the gospel. Dallin H. Oaks observed,

> When someone wanted to do something for my father-in-law but was prevented by circumstances, he would say, "Thank you. I will take the good will for the deed." Similarly, I believe that our Father in Heaven will receive the true desires of our hearts as a substitute for actions that are genuinely impossible.
>
> Here we see another contrast between the laws of God and the laws of men. It is entirely impractical to grant a *legal* advantage on the basis of an intent not translated into action. "I intended to sign that contract," or "We intended to get married," cannot stand as the equivalent of the act required by law. If the law were to give effect to intentions in lieu of specific acts, it would open the door for too much abuse, since the laws of man have no reliable means of determining our inner-most thoughts.
>
> In contrast, the *law of God* can reward a righteous desire because an omniscient God can discern it. As revealed through the prophet of this dispensation, God "is a discerner of the thoughts and intents of the heart" (D&C 33:1). If a person refrains from a particular act because he is genuinely unable to perform it, but truly would if he could, our

Heavenly Father will know this and will reward that person accordingly.[10]

Illustratively, this principle applies to those who seek to marry for eternity but cannot find a suitable partner; to those who desire to serve in callings but are prevented by age or disabilities; and certainly this applies to individuals who are seeking the truths of the restored gospel but "are only kept from the truth because they know not where to find it" (D&C 123:12). Here we begin to see the symbolism: "Because no man hath hired us"—"No one has taught us the gospel. We haven't found it yet, but we are so willing and ready!" Just because some laborers come into the Church later than some lifelong members, we should not conclude that they will deserve less of a reward. "Like other parables, this one can teach several different and valuable principles," declared Dallin H. Oaks. He continued:

> For present purposes its lesson is that the Master's reward in the Final Judgment will not be based on how long we have labored in the vineyard. We do not obtain our heavenly reward by punching a time clock. What is essential is that our labors in the workplace of the Lord have caused us to *become* something. For some of us, this requires a longer time than for others. What is important in the end is what we have become by our labors.
>
> Many who come in the eleventh hour have been refined and prepared by the Lord in ways other than formal employment in the vineyard. These workers are like the prepared dry mix to which it is only necessary to "add water"—the perfecting ordinance of baptism and the gift of the Holy Ghost. With that addition—even in the eleventh hour—these workers are in the same state of development and qualified to receive the same reward as those who have labored long in the vineyard.
>
> This parable teaches us that we should never give up hope and loving associations with family members and friends whose fine qualities . . . evidence their progress toward what a loving Father would have them become. Similarly, the power of the Atonement and the principle of repentance show that we should never give up on loved ones who now seem to be making many wrong choices.
>
> Instead of being judgmental about others, we should be concerned about ourselves. We must not give up hope. We must not stop striving.[11]

We must not forget either that perhaps there are some laborers in God's vineyard, in fact many, who labor for the kingdom without being formal members of the restored Church of Jesus Christ. Ezra Taft Benson said, "God, the Father of us all, uses the men of the earth, especially good men, to accomplish his purposes. It has been true in the past, it is true today, it will be true in the future."[12] Similarly, Orson F. Whitney declared,

> Perhaps the Lord needs such men on the outside of his Church, to help it along. They are among its auxiliaries, and can do more good for the cause where the Lord has placed them, than anywhere else. . . . Hence, some are drawn into the fold and receive a testimony of the truth; while others remain unconverted . . . the beauties and glories of the gospel being veiled temporarily from their view, for a wise purpose. The Lord will open their eyes in his own due time. *God is using more than one people for the accomplishment of his great and marvelous work. The Latter-day Saints cannot do it all. It is too vast, too arduous for any one people.* . . . We have no quarrel with the Gentiles. They are our partners in a certain sense.[13]

The Penny and Pride

Here is another interesting phrase: "When the first came, they supposed that they should have received more." Once again, the thought is ironic and even laughable in light of the symbolism: The penny, as said before, is eternal life—to receive it is, in essence, to receive all that the Father hath (see D&C 84). It is to be a god, thus having all power and all knowledge. It is to have everything. What is the irony then? Simply this—we cannot receive more than eternal life, the greatest of all gifts. One cannot have any more than everything! "Here is your reward—everything!" says the Father. "But I want more!" exclaims the all-day laborer. The mind and heart are truly baffled at the thought. Again we beg to question the true motives of this group that labored all day. It seems that they are not so much concerned with receiving the reward and being content with it, but they simply want to make sure they are ahead of, and always and forever ahead of, those who labored for fewer hours. The focus is on status, not spiritual attainment. C. S. Lewis accordingly observed,

> Pride gets no pleasure out of having something, only out of having more of it than the next man. We say that people are proud of being rich, or clever, or good-looking, but they are not. They are proud of being richer, or cleverer, or better-looking than others. If every one else became equally rich, or clever, or good-looking there would be

nothing to be proud about. It is the comparison that makes you proud: the pleasure of being above the rest. Once the element of competition has gone, pride has gone.[14]

The spirit of entitlement has no place in God's kingdom—either here on earth or in heaven.

Conclusion

The parable of the laborers in the vineyard is a timeless story with deep meaning for those with ears to hear and eyes to see. It is a powerful warning against the spirit of pride and entitlement. Additionally, and more important, it is a potent statement and a sublime testimony regarding the grace, mercy, and awesome power of the atoning sacrifice of our Lord and Savior Jesus Christ. Indeed, it could just well be that the preferred way the Savior chose to teach about the multitudinous principles relating to his infinite Atonement was through the carefully cloaked statements contained in these seemingly simple stories of everyday life. The Lord told Enoch, "All things have their likeness, and all things are created and made to bear record of me, both things which are temporal, and things which are spiritual" (Moses 6:63). So it is with the parables of the laborers in the vineyard.

Notes

1. Bruce R. McConkie, *Mormon Doctrine*, 2nd ed. (Salt Lake City: Bookcraft, 1966), 553.
2. Joseph Smith, *Teachings of the Prophet Joseph Smith*, sel. by Joseph Fielding Smith (Salt Lake City: Deseret Book, 1977), 276–77.
3. Bruce R. McConkie, *Doctrinal New Testament Commentary* (Salt Lake City: Bookcraft, 1970), 1:560–61.
4. Dallin H. Oaks, "What Think Ye of Christ?" *Ensign*, Nov. 1988, 67.
5. Bruce R. McConkie; as quoted in Mark L. McConkie, *Doctrines of the Restoration: Sermons & Writings of Bruce R. McConkie* (Salt Lake City: Bookcraft, 1989), 76.
6. Harry Emerson Fosdick, *Twelve Tests of Character* (1923), 87–88; as quoted in L. Tom Perry, *Ensign*, Nov. 1999, 77.
7. Marion G. Romney, "The Celestial Nature of Self-reliance," *Ensign*, Nov. 1982, 93.
8. Korsaren, *The Forbes Scrapbook of Thoughts on the Business of Life* (New York: Forbes Inc., 1968), 427; as quoted in J. Richard Clarke, "The Value of Work," *Ensign*, May 1982, 78.
9. Boyd K. Packer, *The Holy Temple* (Salt Lake City: Bookcraft, 1980), 58.

10. Dallin H. Oaks, "The Desires of Our Hearts," *Ensign*, June 1986, 66.
11. Dallin H. Oaks, in Conference Report, Oct. 2000, 44.
12. Ezra Taft Benson, *Ensign*, July 1972, 59.
13. Orson F. Whitney, in Conference Report, Apr. 1928, 59; emphasis added.
14. C. S. Lewis, *Mere Christianity* (New York: Collier Books), 109–110.

The Prodigal Son's Identity Restored by the Power of the Perfect Atonement

by Ronald E. Bartholomew

After Moses had beheld the Lord in all his glory, Satan appeared to him, challenging his recently revealed identity. The Lord had said to Moses, "Behold, thou art my son. . . . and thou art in the similitude of mine Only Begotten" (Moses 1:4, 6). However, "Satan came tempting him, saying: Moses, *son of man*, worship me" (Moses 1:12; emphasis added). Fortunately, Moses' recent experience with the Almighty had not completely left him, and he simply replied, "Who art thou? For behold, I am a son of God, in the similitude of his Only Begotten" (Moses 1:13).

Such a triumph over Satan's attempt to destroy the identity of man is, unfortunately, uncommon. Over the past several centuries the false concept of the Trinity has become the orthodox doctrine for the majority of the Christian world. This belief states that "God" consists of the Father, the Son, and the Holy Spirit, but is a single Being who exists, simultaneously and eternally, in one another as a single Divine essence. Therefore, this "God" could not, by any logic or rationale, be the Father of our spirits. Instead, the Orthodox Christian world universally holds to the belief that God is our father only as the creator of the world, and as such, he watches over it as a father would his children. This reduces God to a watchful caretaker, instead of an actual Father, despite numerous biblical references attributing the fatherhood of our spirits to our Heavenly Father. For example, the Lord told Jeremiah: "Before I formed thee in the belly I knew thee; and before thou camest forth out of the womb I sanctified thee, and I ordained thee a prophet unto the nations" (Jeremiah 1:5). This seems to suggest that Jeremiah, as well as the rest of the human family, was with God before he was born and that we were all with him in the premortal world, where we knew him and he knew us.

In terms of his being our actual father, Zechariah recorded that the Lord "formeth the spirit of man within him" (Zechariah 12:1). Paul's teachings coincide with this doctrine. He taught that we are "the offspring of God" (Acts 17:29) and that God is the "father of spirits" (Hebrews 12:9). However, Satan's assertion that not only Moses but also all of humankind are "sons and daughters of men" has become the accepted idea of the Orthodox Christian world. And the Christian world is not alone in this deception. Muslims believe that attributing the identity and attributes of a father to Allah is sacrilege. These, along with other false views of who and what God is, as well as our true relationship to him, have resulted in the truth of our identity as "begotten sons and daughters unto God" (D&C 76:24) becoming completely lost to the world through the ages of the Great Apostasy.

As a result of this, instead of realizing their true and ennobling identity as sons and daughters of Heavenly Father, many in the world have been tempted by Satan to equate their identities with various aspects of their fallen natures. Believing they are mere humans and not children of Deity, men and women are tempted to believe that their identity stems from their temporal natures, instead of their divine natures they inherited from the Father of their spirits. For example, statements such as "I'm fat," "I'm skinny," "I'm beautiful," or "I'm tan" might accurately describe different aspects of a person's temporary nature or state but not their identities as revealed by scriptures and prophets of the Restoration. Even worse aberrations of this are self-indictments such as "I'm bad," "I'm a sinner," or "I'm an alcoholic," leading people to actually identify with both the physical and spiritual consequences of living in a fallen world.

These statements are not only degrading, they have dangerous moral overtones. They confuse a person's *identity* with his or her *condition, or current and temporary state of being*. The Book of Mormon teaches conclusively that our fallen condition and natures are a *state of being*, rather than the defining characteristics of our identity. For example, Mormon recorded that King Benjamin's people "viewed themselves in their own carnal *state*, even less than the dust of the earth" (Mosiah 4:2; emphasis added). After repenting of their sins, these people experienced the joy attending a complete remission of sins, as well as a mighty change in their hearts, which resulted in their exclaiming that they had "no more disposition to do evil, but to do good continually" (Mosiah 5:2). Surely their identities had not changed—rather, their spiritual condition or state had been changed by the miracle of the Atonement through the workings of the Spirit.

Abinadi taught the wicked priests of King Noah that were it not for a Redeemer, all mankind would have forever remained in "their lost and fallen *state*" (Mosiah 16:4; emphasis added). King Mosiah's people understood clearly that before their conversion, the Lamanites were in a "sinful and polluted *state*" (Mosiah 25:11; emphasis added), as were the rebellious Nephites, who were also in a "carnal and sinful *state*" (Mosiah 26:4; emphasis added). Interestingly, many of the Lamanites and Nephites were later redeemed from this temporary state through the missionary efforts of Alma and the sons of Mosiah. Ammon, speaking of himself and others, declared:

Alma 26:17

17 Who could have supposed that our God would have been so merciful as to have snatched us from our awful, sinful, and polluted state?

Surely their characteristics and natures were changed by the power of the Atonement of Jesus Christ. Their temporary fallen natures were changed permanently. Of these converted Lamanites, Mormon declares,

Alma 23:6

6 And as sure as the Lord liveth, so sure as many as believed, or as many as were brought to the knowledge of the truth, through the preaching of Ammon and his brethren, according to the spirit of revelation and of prophecy, and the power of God working miracles in them—yea, I say unto you, as the Lord liveth, as many of the Lamanites as believed in their preaching, and were converted unto the Lord, never did fall away.

The parable of the prodigal son in Luke chapter 15 demonstrates how God's sons and daughters can be lured by Satan to lose sight of their eternal identities because of the more obvious and glaring aspects of their temporary fallen states. In this parable, both sons were deceived this way. Their distorted views of themselves and each other were the result of forgetting who they were ("begotten sons of God") and identifying instead with what they could more readily perceive with their physical senses: their fallen, temporary natures and condition. Happily, this parable also shows a loving father who was able to see past these distorted perceptions and revealed to his two sons the truth about who and what they really were. This chapter will analyze and discuss this beloved parable from this perspective.

In order to bring this analysis more clearly into focus, we will establish a context for this discussion. This context will be a review of the basic doctrines of the Creation, Fall, and Atonement, and the interplay between each of these doctrines as recorded in this parable. This will aid us in bringing to the surface more clearly the truth about the eternal identity of man. It will also reveal how the deceptions of the adversary concerning our eternal identities can be overcome through a correct understanding and application of these three doctrines, especially the Atonement. Because of Jesus Christ, hope and truth about who and what we really are can be restored to each of us despite the more obvious and glaring realities of the Fall.

The Three Pillars of Eternity

Elder Bruce R. McConkie is the one credited with coining the phrase "the three pillars of eternity." He explained which doctrines he was referring to by this phrase when he wrote: "God himself, the Father of us all, ordained and established a plan of salvation whereby his spirit children might advance and progress and become like him. It is the gospel of God, the plan of Eternal Elohim, the system that saves and exalts, and it consists of three things. These three are the very pillars of eternity itself. They are the most important events that ever have or will occur in all eternity. They are the Creation, the Fall, and the Atonement."[1] These three doctrines will be used to establish a framework for our discussion.

The doctrine of the Creation, simply stated, is this: When the Lord appeared to Moses, he referred to him as "my son" and said that he had created him in "the similitude of mine Only Begotten" (Moses 1:6). He taught him that the same was true of all mankind, who had also been created "in mine own image, in the image of mine Only Begotten created I him; male and female created I them" (Moses 2:27). Importantly, he also explained the divine purpose of this creation to Moses: "For behold, this is my work and my glory—to bring to pass the immortality and eternal life of man" (Moses 1:39). These revelations to Moses contain the complete doctrine of the Creation: We are the literal children of God, created in his image with the potential to become like him. These doctrinal truths appear in other scriptures as well. The Psalmist wrote: "Ye are gods"—speaking of our divine potential to become like our Heavenly Father—"and all of you are children of the most High" (Psalm 82:6). To the Romans Paul penned this inspired declaration: "The Spirit itself beareth witness with our spirit, that we are the children of God: And if children, then heirs; heirs of God, and joint-heirs with Christ" (Romans 8:16–17). To the Saints in Galatia he wrote: "And because ye are sons, God hath sent forth the Spirit of his Son into your hearts, crying, Abba, Father. Wherefore thou art no more a servant, but a son; and if a son, then an heir of God through Christ" (Galatians 4:6–7).

All of these scriptural passages bear witness of the simplicity and eternal truth of the doctrine of the Creation. Elder Boyd K. Packer stated it this way: "You are a child of God. He is the father of your spirit. Spiritually you are of noble birth, the offspring of the King of Heaven. Fix that truth in your mind and hold to it. However many generations in your mortal ancestry, no matter what race or people you represent, the pedigree of your spirit can be written on a single line. You are a child of God!"[2]

The doctrine of the Creation defines and establishes our true identity. This doctrine also clearly and solidly establishes the truth about who and what we have always been, are now, and are meant to become in the future.

The doctrine of the Fall, on the other hand, does not define our identity. Rather, it is confined to a description of our current and temporary condition or state of being. The difference between the two is sometimes subtle but always of immense importance. For example, if we say a person is cold, we are not defining their identity; we are describing a temporary state of being in which they currently exist. Similarly, if a person is a sinner, which we all are, that is also a temporary state of being in which we all exist (or at least can and hopefully will be only temporary). It does not accurately describe that person's identity or potential; in fact, it contradicts the definition of their identity according to the doctrine of the Creation. It is therefore critical that we examine the language of Holy Scripture carefully in discerning between man's identity and potential as opposed to their current and temporary condition or state of being.

King Benjamin, Abinadi, and others repeatedly taught that *we* are not carnal, sensual, and devilish by identity, but that we all currently and temporarily exist in a carnal, lost, and fallen *state*. For example, after hearing King Benjamin's recitation of the Angel's words concerning the coming of Christ (see Mosiah 3), his people became acutely aware of "their own carnal *state*, even less than the dust of the earth" (Mosiah 4:2; emphasis added). Abinadi taught the wicked priests of King Noah of their need for the Atonement of Jesus Christ by stating that because of the Fall, "all mankind [became] carnal, sensual, devilish. . . . Thus all mankind were lost; and behold, they would have been endlessly lost were it not that God redeemed his people from their lost and fallen *state*" (Mosiah 16:3–4; emphasis added). In addition, Alma taught that the Fall was the cause of *all* mankind existing in this state or condition *by nature*: "They had become carnal, sensual, and devilish, by nature" (Alma 42:10). Simply stated, the doctrine of the Fall is this: Because of transgression, the conditions of mortality (which include spiritual and physical death)—procreation, testing, trials, sin, and a probationary period of repentance—were brought into the world. Therefore all men inherit this condition by birth, and unless they overcome it, are in a lost, fallen, carnal, sensual, and devilish state by nature, subject unto the devil himself (see also Alma 42:6–27; 2 Nephi 2:21–26; 2 Nephi 9:8–19).

One of the purposes of the doctrine of the Fall is to establish the absolute need for the third pillar of eternity—the doctrine of the Atonement, which for our purposes could be defined this way: Because of the universal fallen nature and condition of all men, a Savior or Redeemer was necessary. If fallen man will come unto Christ with full purpose of heart and work out their salvation with fear and trembling before God (see Mormon 9:27), using their God-given agency to deny themselves of all ungodliness and love God with all their heart, might, mind, and strength, then through his grace they would be able to completely overcome all the effects of the Fall. Moroni taught this beautifully when he wrote:

Moroni 10:32–33   32 Yea, come unto Christ, and be perfected in him, and deny yourselves of all ungodliness; and if ye shall deny yourselves of all ungodliness, and love God with all your might, mind and strength, then is his grace sufficient for you, that by his grace ye may be perfect in Christ; and if by the grace of God ye are perfect in Christ, ye can in nowise deny the power of God.

33 And again, if ye by the grace of God are perfect in Christ, and deny not his power, then are ye sanctified in Christ by the grace of God, through the shedding of the blood of Christ, which is in the covenant of the Father unto the remission of your sins, that ye become holy, without spot.

Alma taught that this would be required for all:

Mosiah 27:25–26

25 Marvel not that all mankind, yea, men and women, all nations, kindreds, tongues and people, must be born again; yea, born of God, changed from their carnal and fallen state, to a state of righteousness. . . .

26 And thus they become new creatures.

He also taught that the powerful effects of the Atonement did not just overcome sin and death, but the other vicissitudes of mortality as well:

Alma 7:11–12

11 And he shall go forth, suffering pains and afflictions and temptations of every kind; and this that the word might be fulfilled which saith he will take upon him the pains and the sicknesses of his people.

12 And he will take . . . upon him their infirmities, that his bowels may be filled with mercy, according to the flesh, that he may know according to the flesh how to succor his people according to their infirmities.

However, we must be proactive if our fallen condition is to be fully overcome by the power of the Atonement. Moroni recorded these words of the Lord to him:

Ether 12:27

27 And if men come unto me I will show unto them their weakness. I give unto men weakness that they may be humble; and my grace is sufficient for all men that humble themselves before me; for if they humble themselves before me, and have faith in me, then will I make weak things become strong unto them.

In fact, Nephi said that the Atonement could only overcome the effects of the Fall "after all we can do" (2 Nephi 25:23). The prophet-recorder Amaleki succinctly and poetically summarized what is required of each of us to benefit from the full effects of the Atonement this way:

Omni 1:26

> **26** And now, my beloved brethren, I would that ye should come unto Christ, who is the Holy One of Israel, and partake of his salvation, and the power of his redemption. Yea, come unto him, and offer your whole souls as an offering unto him, and continue in fasting and praying, and endure to the end; and as the Lord liveth ye will be saved.

The Parable of the Prodigal Son and the Twin Deceptions Regarding Our True Identities

We will now examine this parable in the context of the truths established by these three doctrines. In this story, both sons fall into one of the adversary's most common traps: they confuse their *identity* with their *condition, or current and temporary state of being.* In Luke 15:19 and 21 the returning prodigal denies his identity as a son based on his unworthy condition, or current state of being. He says in both verses that he is "no more worthy to be called [a] son" and proposes returning to his father's household in hopes of being hired as a servant. It appears that he is confusing his fallen nature and condition with his identity as a son. Instead of remembering his unchangeable genealogy, he sees himself as bad, or a sinner, and somehow unworthy to be his father's son. Unfortunately, there are many among us today who make the same mistake. Unable to reconcile the difference between our fallen nature and condition and our eternal identities, we struggle to feel "worthy enough" to go to our father as one of his children.

While it is true that our current condition of worthiness is an important aspect in undergoing the process of spiritual conversion, thus becoming the "begotten sons and daughters of Christ" (see Mosiah 5:7), our identity as "begotten sons and daughters unto God" (D&C 76:24) is the eternal identity of all of Heavenly Father's children—regardless of our current state of worthiness. We are told in D&C 76:24 that all of the inhabitants of this earth are "begotten sons and daughters unto God."

Malachi wrote of this:

Malachi 2:10   10 Have we not all one father? Hath not one God created us?

The Apostle Paul also testified of this truth to those at Ephesus: "We are the offspring of God" (Acts 17:29). Just as the returning prodigal son could not change his identity as his father's son, we cannot change the identity of our spirits as God's begotten sons and daughters. He is our Eternal Father, and we are his children regardless of the mistakes or sins we commit in mortality.

The more faithful son in this parable struggles with these same identity issues in a different way: because he has been more faithful to his father and more consistent in carrying out his duties as a son, he not only fails to see the inherent identity and potential of his brother, but in his pride, he compares his current condition and nature with that of his brother. He actually sees himself as more deserving of the title "son," based on these comparisons. He identified his returning brother by his current sinful condition, while identifying himself by his current self-perceived state of righteousness. When approached by his father, he labels his brother as the one that had "devoured [his father's] living with harlots" (Luke 15:30), while characterizing himself this way:

Luke 15:29   29 These many years do I serve thee, neither transgressed I at any time thy commandment.

While his characterizations are fairly accurate, the insinuation is where the pride is manifest. He is suggesting that the father has erred in celebrating his errant brother's return. Shouldn't his constant presence be more celebrated, based on his "righteousness"? King Benjamin warned us of the evil of comparing our righteousness with another person's sinfulness when he said:

Mosiah 4:17–19   17 Perhaps thou shalt say: The man has brought upon himself his misery; therefore. . . . his punishments are just—
18 But I say unto you, O man, whosoever doeth this the same hath great cause to repent; and except he repenteth of that which he hath done he perisheth forever, and hath no interest in the kingdom of God.

> **19** For behold, are we not all beggars? Do we
> not all depend upon the same Being, even God,
> for all the substance which we have?

President Ezra Taft Benson taught this regarding this ugly deception:

> We are tempted daily to elevate ourselves above others and diminish them (see Helaman 6:17; D&C 58:41).
>
> The proud make every man their adversary by pitting their intellects, opinions, works, wealth, talents, or any other worldly measuring device against others. In the words of C. S. Lewis: "Pride gets no pleasure out of having something, only out of having more of it than the next man. It is the comparison that makes you proud: the pleasure of being above the rest. Once the element of competition has gone, pride has gone" (*Mere Christianity* [New York: Macmillan, 1952], 109–110).[3]

Does the more faithful brother need less of the Atonement than the returning prodigal son? Perhaps he perceives it as such; however, not only are we all beggars, "relying wholly upon the merits of him who is mighty to save" (2 Nephi 31:19), but regardless of how obedient we are, we will always remain indebted to him. We all need 100 percent of the Atonement to be saved. However, this has nothing to do with our eternal identity as his sons and daughters. We are all his children, and we are all completely dependent on his saving grace—regardless of past or current "gospel performance."

Unlike Moses, who was not deceived by Satan's temptation to confuse him regarding his true identity as a son of God, and more like these two brothers and sons, many in our day have also become deceived by Satan's temptation to equate their identity with various aspects of their fallen nature and condition, or to compare their situation to others and be lifted up in false pride. Like the prodigal son, some feel less worthy of their eternal identities. Like the more faithful son, some, unfortunately, feel more worthy of their eternal identity as one of God's children *when comparing themselves* to those who are less faithful, from their perspective. Perhaps the worst effects of these satanic deceptions are the hopelessness it carries with it on the one hand and the false pride it induces on the other. Faith in the Lord Jesus Christ and his perfect, infinite, and eternal Atonement would lead any child of God to realize that all the effects of the Fall can be completely overcome through his Atonement. The

Atonement of Jesus Christ not only overcomes all the effects of the Fall, but it also enables us to realize our potential to become as the Father is—the divine destiny of every child of God.

The Parable of the Apple Tree

Perhaps the phenomenon of confusing our condition with our identity can better be illustrated with a parable. We will compare God to an apple tree. As his offspring, we will compare ourselves, in our fallen, mortal condition, to the apples growing on the tree. The seed inside the apple could be compared to the part of us that has the potential to become like God. No one in mortality can see through our apple exterior to our inner seed except for God. Therefore, the truth about our divine potential remains hidden and covered by our temporary apple exterior.

If the apple tree were growing in a place where it could be untouched by human hands, eventually the apple would fall to the ground. As far as the seed is concerned, the purpose of the apple in that fallen state is to nourish the seed until it gets root and grows into a tree—or, in our analogy, becomes like God.

Our divine destiny and purpose is not to become apples, but to become apple trees. However, in mortality we do not resemble an apple tree at all, or even the seed of an apple tree. All we or other people can see is our outer shell—the apple. Because of this, it is sometimes hard to remember that our divine potential—in fact, our only potential—is to become an apple tree. It is equally difficult to remember other people's seeds, or divine potentials, because all we can see are their apples as well.

This phenomenon leads to one of the most cunning deceptions of the adversary—an inordinate focus of time and energy on making our apple as attractive as possible, or even worse, more attractive than the apples of those around us. This is a cause of pride both ways (looking down and up) and is a great distraction. Satan seduces many to spend more time improving the outward appearance of their temporary apple nature than to developing the seed with infinite potential within. When it is all said and done, our apple will do the same thing everyone else's apple will do—it will die and be laid down to rest in the dust from whence it came.

Our seed, on the other hand, which has the potential to become like our Father—can become a tree that can produce other trees, through the seeds of the fruit of apples, into the eternities. Whenever we judge ourselves or others based on what we can see—the temporary, external apple—instead of what we cannot—the seed—we become victims of the same satanic deceptions the two sons in this parable fell victim to. We either lose hope in the prospects of ever becoming a legitimate and worthy son or daughter of our Heavenly Father, or we are deceived into basing our perceptions of our own "goodness" on the temporary fallen condition of our brothers and sisters.

The Atonement of Jesus Christ Overcomes All the Effects of the Fall

(including the mistaken perceptions of self and others)

What these two sons did not understand about the Savior and the Atonement, their father tried to teach them. Speaking through the father, the Savior taught that our current nature and condition are not the defining aspects of our identity. While returning to his father's house, the prodigal son carefully prepared and recited to himself the speech he planned on using in hopes of being accepted as a servant in his father's house:

Luke 15:18–19   18 I will arise and go to my father, and will say unto him, Father, I have sinned against heaven, and before thee,
19 And am no more worthy to be called thy son: make me as one of thy hired servants.

When his father saw him "yet a great way off," he ran to him and with compassion "fell on his neck and kissed him" (Luke 15:20). Despite his father's warm reception, the son immediately began to recite his carefully, premeditated speech:

Luke 15:21   21 Father, I have sinned against heaven, and in thy sight, and am no more worthy to be called thy son.

However, before he could finish his memorized speech and request a position as a hired servant, his father dismissed his son's misunderstanding about himself and exclaimed:

Luke 15:24   24 For this *my son* was dead, and is alive again; he was lost, and is found. [Emphasis added.]

On the other hand, the more faithful son, upon seeing his father's rejoicing and celebration at the prodigal son's return, was angry and refused to participate. When his father went out to entreat him, the faithful son immediately fell into the pride-trap of comparison:

Luke 15:29–30

29 Lo, these many years do I serve thee, neither transgressed I at any time thy commandment: and yet thou never gavest me a kid, that I might make merry with my friends:
30 But as soon as this thy son was come, which hath devoured thy living with harlots, thou hast killed for him the fatted calf.

His father, in perfect clarity, reminds him of his true, eternal identity as a son and applies that same identity to his brother, saying:

Luke 15:31–32

31 *Son*, thou art ever with me, and all that I have is thine.
32 It was meet that we should make merry, and be glad: for this *thy brother* was dead, and is alive again; and was lost, and is found. [Emphasis added.]

As Elder Lynn A. Mickelsen taught: "In the parable of the prodigal son, the prodigal was reclaimed by a faithful father who spoke of his son's worth, not of his faults."[4]

Similarly, when any prodigal child completes the journey back to his Father, his knowledge of and belief in his true identity can be restored. He or she is, and always will be, a child of God. Our identity as his begotten sons and daughters is not based on worthiness, but on lineage. He is, and will always be, the Father of our eternal spirits. Likewise, our pride and arrogance do not remove the eternal identity of our erring brothers and sisters. Fortunately, our pride does not alter our eternal identity either.

Therefore, a correct understanding of the doctrines of the Creation, Fall, and Atonement allow us to place this story in a helpful doctrinal framework: (1) the doctrine of the Creation establishes the truth that both the prodigal son and his more faithful brother's eternal, unchanging identities were "son," each being created in his father's image, with the potential to become like him; (2) the doctrine of the Fall implies that both of their mortal natures and conditions (both were sinful in very different ways) could be temporary states of being; and (3) the doctrine of the Atonement bears witness that if either or both of them were to apply unto the Savior and his Atonement in faith, they could be forgiven and have their natures and conditions changed (see Mosiah 2:3, where King Benjamin's people plead for the application of the atoning blood of Christ for both forgiveness and a change in their natures). In fact, they can both become as their father is.

What hope is there for returning prodigals? Upon the son's return, how is he accepted—as a son or a servant? Falling into mud does not change your identity, regardless of how long you stay in it. True, the longer you immerse yourself in it the more extensive will be the process of extracting yourself from it and eventually becoming clean. However, you would not turn into mud unless you died in it, at which time the scriptural injunction "for dust thou art, and unto dust thou shalt return" (Genesis 3:19) would eventually apply. Similarly, sinning does not and cannot change you into a sinner, unless, like in the example of the mud, you die in your sins. As Elder Neal A. Maxwell pointed out in regard to the returning prodigal: "The prophet Mormon at first thought his people were sorrowing unto repentance (see Mormon 2:12–13). Yet he soon discerned that theirs was not actually the sorrowing unto repentance but the sorrowing of the damned, stranding them in a no-man's-land. Compare that episode to the prodigal son's solitary working through of his own repentance; since his sorrow was real, he truly 'came to himself.' "[5] If, like the prodigal son, one "comes to himself" before it is too late (see Amulek's plea in Alma 34:33–35), then the power of the Atonement will have its full effect in reclaiming and restoring such a prodigal.

Of the mistaken idea that for the repentant prodigal it is somehow too late, President Boyd K. Packer said, "Letters come from those who have made tragic mistakes. They ask, 'Can I *ever* be forgiven?' The answer is *yes!* The gospel teaches us that relief from torment and guilt can be earned through repentance. Save for those few who defect to perdition after having known a fullness, there is no habit, no addiction, no rebellion, no transgression, no offense exempted from the promise of complete forgiveness."[6] He also said:

> It is a wicked, wicked world in which we live and in which our children must find their way. Challenges of pornography, gender confusion, immorality, child abuse, drug addiction, and all the rest are everywhere. There is no way to escape from their influence.
>
> Some are led by curiosity into temptation, then into experimentation, and some become trapped in addiction. They lose hope. . . .
>
> The angels of the devil convince some that they are born to a life

from which they cannot escape and are compelled to live in sin. The most wicked of lies is that they cannot change and repent and that they will not be forgiven. That cannot be true. They have forgotten the Atonement of Christ.

"For, behold, the Lord your Redeemer suffered death in the flesh; wherefore he suffered the pain of all men, that all men might repent and come unto him" (D&C 18:11).

Christ is the Creator, the Healer. What He made, He can fix. The gospel of Jesus Christ is the gospel of repentance and forgiveness (see 2 Ne. 1:13; 2 Ne. 9:45; Jacob 3:11; Alma 26:13–14; Moro. 7:17–19).[7]

Similarly, there is hope for the self-perceived faithful who have fallen into the trap of false pride. The purpose of the Atonement of Jesus Christ is to overcome all the effects of the Fall, including our false perceptions about ourselves and others.

Notes
1. Bruce R. McConkie, "Christ and the Creation," *Ensign*, June 1982, 9.
2. Boyd K. Packer, in Conference Report, Apr. 1989, 71.
3. Ibid., 4.
4. Lynn A. Mickelsen, in Conference Report, Oct. 2003, 10.
5. Neal A. Maxwell, in Conference Report, Apr. 2000, 91.
6. Boyd K. Packer, in Conference Report, Oct. 1995, 22.
7. Boyd K. Packer, in Conference Report, Apr. 2006, 28.

"Because Thou Desiredst Me"

The Greatness and Mercy of Our God
Matthew 18:23–35

by R. Scott Burton

The Immediate Context of the Parable

$\mathcal{T}$he Prophet Joseph Smith offered this rule of thumb for the interpretation of scripture in general, and the parables of Jesus in particular: "I have a key by which I understand the scriptures. I enquire, what was the question which drew out the answer, or caused Jesus to utter the parable? . . . To ascertain its meaning, we must dig up the root and ascertain what it was that drew the saying out of Jesus."[1]

What, then, was the question that caused Jesus to utter the parable of the unmerciful servant?[2] The answer is not hard to find.

Matthew 18:21	21 Then came Peter to him, and said, Lord, how oft shall my brother sin against me, and I forgive him? till seven times?

The issue is one that humans have dealt with since Eden, I suppose. How should we respond to the sins and offenses—real or imagined, intentional or accidental—that are committed against us? Now, Jesus is very realistic about the existence of such sins and offenses: "It must needs be that offenses come."

So the question is by no means theoretical. It is real and deadly serious. The primary questions that Jesus' parable of the unmerciful servant

31

seeks to answer are: "In responding to offense, just how forgiving must we be?" and "In respect to forgiveness, just how magnanimous must we be?"

The Extended Context of the Parable

While the prophet's "key" of looking at the immediate context in order to understand the scriptures is wise and effective (to say nothing of modern), it may be too great a restriction to limit our interpretation to this immediate context. Within Matthew's narrative, it seems that there is a wider context and a second, related question that informs the parable and our interpretation of it. Identifying the extended context for any passage can be a rather arbitrary and even subjective enterprise. How far backward and how far forward in the text does one go? Often, a context is identified that meets a preconceived notion. All one can do is be as transparent as possible about one's intent.

In the present case, from the narrative's standpoint Jesus was in Capernaum when he delivered the parable.[3] He had "come to Capernaum" with his disciples in Matthew 17:24. In looking for an extended context, this is as far backward in the text as we shall go. In Matthew 19:1, Jesus "departed from Galilee, and came into the coasts of Judea beyond Jordan." This is as far forward in the text as we will go.[4] Thus, we will treat Matthew 17:24–18:35 as the extended context of the parable.

In this section, we have, principally, two episodes. In the first, Peter is challenged as to his master's "patriotism": "Doth not your master pay tribute?" (Matthew 17:24). Peter defends his master by assuring government officials that Jesus did indeed pay tribute, and thus demonstrated allegiance to the powers that be. Jesus gently and diplomatically corrects Peter's false pretension but offers a solution to a potential "political" stand-off (see Matthew 17:25–27).

In the second episode, the disciples ask a question that is often at the forefront of human thought: "Who is the greatest?" (see Matthew 18:1). In responding to this question, Jesus reviews the attribute of humility with his disciples (see 18:2–5). This discussion about humility is then closely tied to the problem of offense (see 18:6–9). The discussion about offense is tightly connected to Jesus' calling to "save that which [is] lost"—i.e. he has solutions to the problem of omnipresent and inevitable offense (18:10–14). Finally, Jesus connects all of this with the issue of how we are to deal with sin and offense (see 18:15–22). This precipitates Peter's question that "draws" our parable from Jesus.

Peter's question about the extent of forgiveness, then, is asked in the context of the first question, "Who is the greatest?" Now, it is certainly true that we can positively frame this first question so that Peter seeks simply to know, "What does it mean to be 'great'?" The Savior will indeed devote a great deal of instructional time to this question. In addition, he will answer this question by his own actions. As we shall see, the parable of the unmerciful servant surely describes at least one attribute of greatness—a forgiving disposition.

However, the question can also be framed less innocently: "How do I exert my superiority over others?" This question has been posed since the dawn of time. It is at the very heart of the conflict between Cain and Abel. It is at the very center of most human conflict. It is a recurring cause of offense. Lest we imagine that this negative formation of the question could be nowhere present in the mind of the Apostles, we should remind ourselves of another episode. Very shortly after our current passage, the narrative informs us that the mother of James and John made a special request of Jesus.

Matthew 20:21	21 Grant that these my two sons may sit, the one on thy right hand, and the other on the left, in thy kingdom.

This is a reformulation of the earlier question: "Who is the greatest?" The text informs us that "when the ten heard it, they were moved with indignation against the two brethren" (Matthew 20:24). Jesus then had to lecture the Apostles once more on the nature of true greatness (see Matthew 20:25–28).

There is a very close and highly significant relationship between greatness and forgiveness. The parable of the unmerciful servant explores this relationship. These, then, are the issues, the questions (immediate and extended), that "drew the saying out of Jesus" and "caused Jesus to utter the parable" of the unmerciful servant.

The Theological Context of the Parable

In a 1999 conference talk, Elder Russell M. Nelson, speaking specifically about the Book of Mormon, counseled, "Study of the Book of Mormon is most rewarding when one focuses on its *primary* purpose—to testify of Jesus Christ. By comparison, all other issues are incidental. When you read the Book of Mormon, concentrate on the principal figure in the book—from its first chapter to the last—the Lord Jesus Christ, Son of the Living God."[5]

This is wise counsel. It simply does not pay to allow "incidental" issues to dominate "primary" issues. Lehi's vision of the tree of life, as Nephi quickly discovered, was not about iron rods, great and spacious buildings, or mists of darkness—incidentals, all. Like a laser beam, the Spirit focused Nephi's mind on the dream's central character—the tree. The subject and focus of this dream was to be the love of God, expressed most clearly and powerfully through the gift of Jesus Christ and his infinite Atonement.

Elder Nelson's counsel could apply equally well, perhaps even more so, to the entire New Testament, with the Gospels holding a special and prominent place even within that canon. As we read the Gospels, we should concentrate on the principal figure. Luke did not record the Savior's encounter with "Legion," for example, in order for us to focus on the phenomenon of possession. And certainly the story was not about pigs! (I've often wondered whether Luke, observing how often we become fascinated and fixated on the herd of pigs running over a cliff to be drowned, might, if he had it to do over again, leave the pigs out of the story entirely.) No indeed, Luke would have us focus on Jesus and the dramatic impact his ministry of healing and redemption had upon a very, very disturbed and oppressed man.

While the immediate and extended context of the parable under discussion is important for interpretive purposes, it would seem, again, unwise to end there. Mormon and Moroni remind us that authors and editors have points of view. They utilize stories and narratives to emphasize and teach certain perspectives. Mormon and Moroni were determined to "edit for Christ."[6] Like them, Matthew, as a gifted and inspired editor, has questions, issues, emphases, themes, and perspectives that he wants to examine. He will return to them over and over. It would not, then, be inappropriate to read this, or any other parable, in light of Matthew's larger purposes.

So, in addition to setting the parable within its immediate and extended context, Matthew also would have wanted it to contribute to the central message of his entire work. He would have wanted it to confirm the primary purpose of his Gospel—to testify that Jesus is the Christ. He would have wanted to focus the mind of his reader not only upon the *teachings* of the Master, but upon *the Master himself.* We should not be surprised, then, to find that, notwithstanding Peter's anthropological question—"how oft shall . . . I forgive?"—the answering parable is not only, or even primarily, anthropological. The anthropological question will be answered with a theological assertion. It is this theological assertion that gives power to the anthropological challenge: "Therefore is *the kingdom of heaven* likened unto a certain king" (Matthew 18:23; emphasis added).

The Kingdom of Heaven and a Certain King

This, then, is how our parable begins: "Therefore is the kingdom of heaven likened unto a certain king." The reader should note that the kingdom of heaven is "likened unto a certain *king*," not "likened unto a certain *citizen*." No doubt Jesus could have told a parable about really spectacular citizens of heaven's kingdom—marvelous in their capacities to forgive. He could have spoken of the sociological, psychological, spiritual, and societal advantages that come to individuals and groups as they forgive. Surely, if mankind followed Jesus' teachings from only such a perspective, life on planet earth would be vastly different and significantly improved. But the parable is bigger than this.

Our attention is drawn first and foremost *not* to the kingdom's citizens—and not even to our proverbial unmerciful servant—but to its king. The parable is about a king first, a debtor second. And the king is no ordinary king, for he is likened to the kingdom of heaven. The king is a divine king. If we are unsure of this as we read the parable, Jesus clears matters up nicely as he makes application for his disciples. "So likewise shall my heavenly Father do" (Matthew 18:35). The parable, then, gives us a glimpse into the workings of heaven and the attributes of its sovereign Lord.

Jesus presents us with a theological certainty that shapes and determines our own anthropological behavior. Whatever the answer to Peter's question about forgiving may be, it is based upon the character of God. The parable isn't only about how men become good men. It isn't only about the human quality and application of forgiveness. It is about God himself. And so, in the parable Jesus draws us a little sketch of God—about "what kind of a being God is." The reader is, no doubt, aware that this quotation comes from one of the Prophet Joseph Smith's greatest challenges.

> I want to ask this congregation, every man, woman and child, to answer the question in their own heart, what kind of a being God is?

Ask yourselves; turn your thoughts into your hearts, and say if any of you have seen, heard, or communed with him. This is a question that may occupy your attention for a long time. I again repeat the question: What kind of a being is God? Does any man or woman know? Have any of you seen him, heard him, or communed with him? Here is the question that will, peradventure, from this time henceforth occupy your attention.[7]

We do not, then, in any way stretch the bounds of propriety if we explore the parable in order to understand both the *teachings* of the master (in this case, his teachings about forgiveness) *and the Master himself*—what kind of being is he?[8] God's character is fundamental to our own desires for something higher in ourselves. This parable specifically instructs us about the king's—i.e., God's—willingness to forgive, or his forgiving disposition. This beautiful phrase is also from the Prophet Joseph.[9]

Unless [God] was merciful and gracious, slow to anger, long-suffering and full of goodness, such is the weakness of human nature, and so great the frailties and imperfections of men, that unless they believed that these excellencies existed in the divine character, the faith necessary to salvation could not exist; for doubt would take the place of faith, and those who know their weakness and liability to sin would be in constant doubt of salvation if it were not for the idea which they have of the excellency of the character of God, that he is slow to anger and long-suffering, and of a *forgiving disposition*, and does forgive iniquity, transgression, and sin. An idea of these facts does away doubt, and makes faith exceedingly strong.[10]

Those of us who are parents know a little something about dispositions. We could speak about the disposition of each of our children. One is happy-go-lucky. One is sober and anxious. And what of God's disposition? In an attempt to get right to the very heart of God, to capture the very essence of his being, the Prophet chose to speak of him as being disposed to forgive. Those of us who are parents have learned and are learning something about this as well. Our Father's natural inclination—his first response to sin, weakness, folly, foible, error, transgression, and so forth—is to forgive.

Our parable of the unmerciful servant is, then, first about God. It powerfully affirms the divine attribute, the divine disposition to forgive, and surprises us with its expansiveness. Oh, how expansive it is!

The Parable's Intimidating Arithmetic and Its Message

Matthew 18:21   21 Lord, how oft shall my brother sin against me, and I forgive him? Till seven times?

In posing his question, Peter undoubtedly thought himself most expansive and magnanimous. He was, after all, willing to consider the possibility of forgiving someone up to seven whole times! Before launching into the parable itself, Jesus answers Peter's question with this shocking and bubble-popping assertion: We are to forgive seventy *times* seven (see Matthew 18:22). One senses that this assertion should be followed by about a dozen increasingly bold exclamation points! Of course, the point is not that we keep track of offenses against us up to 490, forgiving all along the way. The point is that we never stop forgiving. We might be forgiven if, at times, we find this expectation offensive!

In slightly different phrasing, but with the same point in mind, Luke records Jesus' instruction to his disciples that "if [thy brother] trespass against thee seven times in a day, and seven times in a day turn again to thee, saying, I repent; thou shalt forgive him" (Luke 17:4).[11] This time our text *is* followed by a huge *verbal* exclamation point: "Lord, Increase our faith" (Luke 17:5). Whether it is seven times in a day or seventy times seven, it is simply asking too much! The Apostles recognize that they are not up to the challenge. They will need help.

The question might be asked, "Is *anyone* up to the challenge?" The parable boldly answers in the affirmative by introducing the second intimidating number: ten thousand talents. This represents an amount of personal debt our divine King forgave a "servant" debtor. The text does not indicate, specifically, whether the debt of ten thousand talents was in gold, silver, something else, or some combination. We need not become overly concerned with the question. However, to give some idea about the amount owed we can note that the servant's debt probably amounted to something between one hundred million and five billion dollars by today's standards. By any day's standards "ten thousand talents" is a huge, likely debilitating and impossibly high amount to pay off.

We meet a servant, then, who is in debt to the tune of an incredible, let's say, five billion dollars. How very foolish a man he must have been! We can't think of him as simply having been suddenly caught up in a momentary and unwise choice. Such a debt does not accumulate overnight. He's been at it for some time. He's had plenty of time to consider the consequences. Why didn't he stop borrowing long ago? He must have known that he would never be able to pay off such a debt. What kind of brazenness is this? When the time of reckoning finally arrives, we are not surprised to find that "he had not to pay."

Now, we ask, is there a message in the arithmetic? It seems that there is. If Jesus simply wanted to teach his Apostles about the importance of forgiving others, any amount would have done the trick. But Jesus does not, in fact, only answer the questions that are asked. He also answers the questions that might and should be asked, and those that most desperately need to be answered. Jesus can do more than one thing at a time.[12] What is the secondary teaching? Before there can be forgiveness, there is the *need* for forgiveness. There is *recognition* of a debt. Jesus has something to say about human debt before God.

Millennia before the Savior's earthly ministry, a man in need made a startling and candid confession in prayer:

Ether 3:2   2 We know that thou art holy and dwellest in the heavens, and that we are unworthy before thee; because of the fall our natures have become evil continually.

This speaks to the same debt acquired by our proverbial servant. Centuries later, Nephi, in describing one of life's greatest joys, spoke of this same debt like this:

2 Nephi 11:6   6 My soul delighteth in proving unto my people that save Christ should come all men must perish.

Several more centuries would pass before the great Book of Mormon missionary, Aaron, would declare, with uncompromising directness, this unavoidable verdict:

Alma 22:14   14 Since man had fallen he could not merit anything of himself.

Two or three decades after the Savior's earthly ministry, Paul would describe this same debt with unparalleled succinctness:

Romans 3:23   23 All have sinned, and come short of the glory of God.

Jesus teaches his ancient listening audience and his modern reading audience a profound truth about the Fall and its debilitating effects upon all. All incur a huge debt to God. All incur a debt that is, and ever will be, impossible to pay off. The extreme amount of the man's debt is uncompromising. It leaves us no out. It can't be shrugged off as insignificant. The Apostle Paul would later quote the Old Testament, with an equally poignant contention.

Romans 3:10–12, 19

10 There is none righteous, no, not one:

11 There is none that understandeth, there is none that seeketh after God.

12 They are all gone out of the way, they are together become unprofitable; there is none that doeth good, no, not one. . . .

19 Now we know that what things soever the law saith, it saith to them who are under the law: that every mouth may be stopped, and *all* the world may become guilty before God. [Emphasis added.]

So it is that the parable's arithmetic teaches us of our fall and our incalculable debt. It is a debt, in fact, that is beyond our capacities to recompense. We are in deep waters, here. There is no getting out on our own. This is the parable's first revelation. If redemption is to be found, this must be *life's* first revelation.

Ezra Taft Benson said, "Just as a man does not really desire food until he is hungry, so he does not desire the salvation of Christ until he knows why he needs Christ. No one adequately and properly knows why he needs Christ until he understands and accepts the doctrine of the Fall and its effects upon all mankind."[13]

The Parable's Search for Mercy

What is to be done in the face of this debilitating debt? Let's allow the foolish debtor to mark the way.

Matthew 18:26

26 The servant therefore fell down, and worshipped him, saying, Lord, have patience with me, and I will pay thee all.

From one perspective, this is a very nice sentiment: "I will pay thee all." I'm sure he meant it. But really now, the notion is ridiculous. He is not capable of repaying the debt. Even if he were to serve him with his whole soul, yet would he be an unprofitable servant (see Mosiah 2:21). The king will not make a profit on this fellow. He will not even get back what he has invested. The servant would have been wiser, perhaps, and surely more accurate, to confess,

Psalm 38:4   4 Mine iniquities are gone over mine head: as an heavy burden they are too heavy for me.

Perhaps he might have exclaimed,

Psalm 40:12   12 Mine iniquities have taken hold upon me, so that I am not able to look up; they are more than the hairs of mine head.

But we cannot gainsay the wisdom of the servant's plea for patience. This plea for patience, this cry for mercy, is fundamental. It is, in fact, at the very heart of what it means to repent. Alma admonishes his Zoramite audience to "exercise your faith unto repentance." He then clarifies and amplifies what this means and how it looks: "that ye begin to call upon his holy name, that he would have mercy upon you" (Alma 34:17).

We witness this repentance process in action when, finding himself "for the space of many hours in darkness," Lehi "began to pray unto the Lord that he would have mercy on me, according to the multitude of his tender mercies" (1 Nephi 8:8). This simple act of incredible faith, this trust in the goodness of God, this call for mercy led to Lehi's release from the darkness and his discovery of a tree with fruit "desirable above all other" (1 Nephi 8:12). And who could forget Alma's heartfelt and effective repentance when, in his most extreme moment, he gave voice to his most personal and consuming plea: "O Jesus, thou Son of God, have mercy on me" (Alma 36:18).

Oh yes, there will be much to learn and much to do later in hopes of bringing forth "fruits worthy of repentance" (Luke 3:8). We will hope our humble efforts to follow and obey him and his example might be at least proximate to the immeasurable worth of the Lord's plenteous mercy. But this is an outflow from our repentance and forgiveness, not a prerequisite. For now, at the beginning of the intimidating revelation of indebtedness, nothing yields more relief than this repentant inquiry after the merciful God with his forgiving disposition.

If this sounds too easy . . . well, looking upon the serpent appeared too easy for rebellious Israelites bitten and poisoned with sin. And so, "because of the *simpleness* of the way, or the *easiness* of it, there were many who perished" (1 Nephi 17:41; emphasis added). The trust necessary to utter this cry for mercy is extraordinary. It is far from common. Though James tried to teach us to the contrary, we fear that God might "upbraid"[14] (see James 1:5). But we must trust in his forgiving disposition. We must learn what the Savior himself meant when he answered the crowd's question:

John 6:28	28 What shall we do, that we might work the works of God?

His answer is severely challenging:

John 6:29	29 This is the work [and it is a work!] of God, that ye believe on him whom he hath sent.

Some years ago as I read the Book of Mormon I came to Zenock's startling and prayerful confession: "Thou art angry, O Lord, with this people, because . . ." (Alma 33:16). Somehow, I felt moved to stop reading. The Spirit suggested that I complete the sentence myself. I wrote a conclusion. I felt prompted to write another. I wrote another, then another, and another—

Mosiah 4:29	29 I cannot tell you all the things whereby ye may commit sin; for there are divers ways and means, even so many that I cannot number them.

So I discovered and recorded many ways to finish the sentence. I identified a host of reasons why the Lord might be angry with his people.

Having finished my Spirit-led catechism, I was taken back to the text and directed to read the prophetic ending: "because they will not understand thy mercies which thou has bestowed upon them because of thy Son." I was stupefied. I went back to my full page of conclusions. I searched frantically to find this conclusion. It was nowhere to be found. I'm not sure that if I had been given a chance to write a book-length manuscript on the question, it would have made an appearance. I did not possess the prophetic mind, let alone the "mind of Christ" (see 1 Corinthians 2:16). How embarrassing! How shameful! How faithless! Gratefully, I have come to know a little better.

The Parable's Discovery of the Mercy
and Greatness of God

Having listened in on the debtor's sincere plea, we are privileged—and amazed beyond words—to look in on the miracle of forgiveness.

Matthew 18:27   27 Then the lord of that servant was moved with compassion, and loosed him, and forgave him the debt.

2 Nephi 9:19   19 O the greatness of the mercy of our God, the Holy One of Israel!

This unbelievably threatening debt is forgiven in a flood of compassion. Debt, sin, error, weakness; none of them stand a chance in the face of the king's compassion and power—in the face of his "forgiving disposition" and "his grace and truth."

Do we really dare hope for so much? Just how far God is willing to go, just how much he is willing to give, just how much he is willing to do is beyond reckoning.

Alma 26:16–17   16 Who can say too much of his great power, and of his mercy, and of his long-suffering towards the children of men? Behold, I say unto you, I cannot say the smallest part which I feel. 17 Who could have supposed that our God would have been so merciful.

We are constantly underestimating his capacity for patience, long-suffering, and forgiveness. We can hardly "comprehend . . . what is the breadth, and length, and depth, and height" of "the love of Christ" (see Ephesians 3:18–19). Indeed he "is able to do exceeding abundantly above all that we ask or think" (Ephesians 3:20). We strain to comprehend, to paraphrase the Psalmist, that the Lord's mercy is as high as the heaven is above the earth (see Psalm 103:11).

Psalm 103:12   12 As far as the east is from the west, so far hath he removed our transgressions from us.

How high is that, anyway? How far out there do the heavens extend? Can any man measure it? And how far *is* the east from the west? Let's get out our measuring rods and see if we can measure it! But the parable's debt-ridden servant knows. And because of him, so too do we. Through the king's patience and compassion and loosening and forgiving, he and we comprehend, still imperfectly, the measure, the breadth, the length, the depth, the height: an impossible five billion dollars' worth!

With Enos we might ask, "Lord, how is it done?" (Enos 1:7). How and why do you forgive so? The debtor is told quite clearly that he was forgiven "because thou desiredst." The debtor was forgiven his debt because he desired. Our desires mean something to this great and incredibly good-willed God. The debtor asked and was answered. The debtor knocked and it was opened. The debtor sought, and he found. God loves to give. He loves to serve. He loves us. He lives to give and serve and love.

And God is and does all of this because that is the kind of being he is, because of the qualities that reside within his own being, because of his own excellencies. He himself declares that when he forgives, he forgives first "for mine own sake" (read: "consistent with who and what I am").

Isaiah 43:25   25 I, even I, am he that blotteth out thy transgressions for mine own sake [read: "because that's simply the kind of Being I am"], and will not remember thy sins.

The Psalmist came to know and depend upon this truth about the quality and excellency of God.

Psalm 25:7, 11   7 Remember not the sins of my youth, nor my transgressions: according to thy mercy remember thou me for thy goodness' sake, O Lord. . . .
11 For thy name's sake, O Lord, pardon mine iniquity; for it is great.

However great the sin, however massive the debt, there is none so large and powerful that God cannot forgive—provided, of course, that we are willing and that we ask.

D&C 122:8   8 The Son of Man hath descended below them all.

The Parable's Concluding Lessons

"Who is the greatest?" "How oft shall my brother sin against me, and I forgive him?" They seemed such simple and straightforward questions.

Yet, in answering them, Jesus ranged through the universe.

"Who is the greatest?" God is the greatest. He is magnificent beyond our wildest imaginings. Think of it—ten thousand talents! What does greatness look like? Has there ever been, can there ever be a greater, a clearer revelation of greatness than that found in the excruciating pain of Gethsemane? What does a God look like in his greatness? Has there ever been, can there ever be a clearer revelation of God than that found on the agonizing Cross of Calvary? Is there any greatness that surpasses the willingness and capacity to forgive? Might this be, at least in part, what it means to be God?[15]

The somewhat sober theological magnificence of God's forgiving disposition has anthropological implications for each of us. "How oft shall my brother sin against me, and I forgive him?" The anthropological command to forgive "until seventy times seven"—to never quit forgiving—is based upon the theological fact that God forgives seventy times seven—he never quits forgiving. We are called upon to hear and accept this near unbelievable message. We are called upon to accept his immeasurable gift of forgiveness. We are not to "refuse to be comforted" (Moses 7:44).

The servant seems to have accepted the theological truth about God. He experienced the incomparable greatness and mercy of God. It is this that makes his unwillingness to forgive a pittance all the more painful to behold and all the more serious in its repercussions. Having received this priceless gift, he and we are to give in kind. We are called upon to follow our Lord and Savior. We are to imitate him. We are to strive to acquire the very same forgiving disposition that he possesses.

Matthew 18:33   33 Shouldest not thou also have had compassion on thy fellowservant, even as I had pity on thee?

This is what greatness looks like. This is what the greatness of God looks like. This is what it means to truly be God. These truths are fundamental to the message of Jesus' parable of the merciful king.

Notes
1. Joseph Smith, *History of The Church of Jesus Christ of Latter-day Saints*, ed. by B. H. Roberts (Salt Lake City: The Church of Jesus Christ of Latter-day Saints), 5:261.
2. In referring to this parable, I shall use the traditional title, parable of the unmerciful servant. However, Jesus did not title his parables,

and this parable could just as well be called the parable of the merciful king.

3. For our purposes, we need not be much concerned with the historical question, was this parable really (and only) delivered at Capernaum? It's an interesting question, and not in any way unworthy of consideration. But Matthew has a story to tell, and he may, if he chooses, adjust the story's historicity to fit the points he is trying to make. Whether or not he did this—here or otherwise—I'll leave to the reader to decide. From the standpoint of the narrative, the parable is delivered at Capernaum.

4. There are certainly things before and after our cut-off points that might inform our parable. There are things in Alma that might inform our parable! One simply must cut things off in a reasonable fashion, and limiting ourselves to this particular stay in Capernaum does not seem altogether unreasonable.

5. Russell M. Nelson, in Conference Report, Oct. 1999, 86–87.

6. Outside of the title page itself, this is perhaps nowhere more evident than in the Words of Mormon, verses 3–5. Here Mormon informs us of his over-riding objective in the editorial process.

7. *Teachings of the Prophet Joseph Smith*, 343–44.

8. Given the New Testament's constant contention that Jesus and his Father are one, we in no way abuse the text or its message to speak of Father and Son almost interchangeably. Whatever the Father does, Jesus does. Whatever Father thinks, Jesus thinks. However Father responds to a given stimuli, Jesus responds in exactly the same way. This is why we can say and know for a certainty that if Father had been living and walking in Judea of AD 33, if Father had been present during Passover of AD 33, he would be have been found in exactly the same place doing exactly the same thing Jesus was doing on Passover Eve—he would have been hanging on a cross to express his love and unity and oneness with all mankind!

9. It is true that the exact genesis of the *Lectures on Faith*, in whole and in part, is unclear. However, I make the assumption that that which the prophet did not write himself, he was aware of and approved, at least provisionally.

10. *Lectures on Faith*, comp. by N. B. Lundwall (Salt Lake City: Bookcraft, 1985), 3:121–22; emphasis added.

11. I can almost hear a certain portion of the population respond with, "Well! If the man had truly repented he wouldn't have done it a second time—forgiveness is, after all, total and immediate forsaking—let alone seven times in a day." Oh, how little we sometimes understand the foolishness and frailties of mortals! Oh, how well our Savior does understand!

12. There is no better example, perhaps, than that of the parable of the good Samaritan. Jesus did answer the immediate question as to who

is our neighbor. In doing so, however, he chose characters—priest, Levite, and Samaritan—that would allow him to also comment on the sorry state of current, legalistic religion. It had morphed into a religion with doctrines and principles that essentially made it impossible for adherents—even the most prestigious and representative examples—to act in basic and humane ways.

13. Ezra Taft Benson, *A Witness and a Warning: A Modern-Day Prophet Testifies of the Book of Mormon* (Salt Lake City: Deseret Book, 1988), 33.

14. I have suggested elsewhere that the principle that came with such power to the heart of Joseph was not so much that God answers prayers, but that God does not upbraid or scold those who lack wisdom, i.e., those who are inadequate to a task.

15. We often speak of our potential to become "like God." Some even will speak of becoming a God. We speak of it, sometimes, as though it were glorious and beautify and "happifying"—to use a Brigham Young word. Families are forever. One eternal FHE! There is, of course, a truth to all of this. And yet, I am sobered when I see what being a God meant to Jesus. And I wonder.

THE PARABLE OF THE TEN VIRGINS

by Robert England Lee

A Fresh Look at Old Things

Reading the scriptures is an act of faith. We engage in this practice with the hope that by so doing there will come a lift from the burdens of normal life, that there will be a sustaining power to counterbalance the withering relentlessness of mortality. When we walk upon the familiar ground of scripture stories and passages there comes a warmth to our souls, like an encounter with an old friend not seen in ages. Such is the case with the parable of the ten virgins. Notwithstanding the archaic English words and phrases, we feel at home, secure, comfortable. The parable is powerful in its simplicity. Five virgins were wise. (We admire them and secretly identify ourselves with them because of their wisdom.) Five were foolish. (We shake our heads and marvel that they would be so ill prepared.) They all "went forth to meet the bridegroom."

Before we have finished reading the thirteen verses that make up this all too familiar tale, we have raced ahead in our minds, rushing over the words, the words we have read or heard about a thousand times. The resources connected to this parable are staggering. There are even paintings now, and commentary that would fill a rich man's library. And all of this for thirteen verses.

These resources only serve to amplify our familiarity. However, such familiarity has its pitfalls. Take, for example, the way we mark scriptures. Marks on a scripture page made as a young missionary remind you of thoughts you had all those years ago. Yet, those same marks may actually be a block to new thoughts that have been waiting anxiously to break through this impregnable wall of familiarity. That which we read or experience or discover in our youth waits to be reexamined, reexperienced, and rediscovered, as if for the first time, in our maturity. The message in the passages alters over time through the influence of the Holy Ghost to fit our new, pressing need; and to fill our new, larger cup of desire.

I remember as a boy walking the green grass of Gettysburg, the site of the great battle of the War Between the States. In that long-ago walk my young mind could only appreciate the relative antiquity of the cannons and the spectacle of the statues celebrating heroes and their deeds. I walked that same grassy, hallowed ground many years later, as a grandfather. The endless rows of grave-markers summoned emotions vastly different from what I felt as a teenager. The scene produced feelings of profound sadness, not the youthful delight in seeing a cannon. It was a sadness that washed over my soul as I thought of the blood of thousands of soldiers, most of them barely boys, a concourse of young people and fathers who would never see their parents and children again. During this later visit I wept like a little child.

There is something profoundly significant about walking over familiar ground with a new perspective that makes the walk more sacred, more poignant, more important in the here and now.

Even a parable as familiar as the ten virgins may seem even more relevant to our own here and now with a careful reexamination. And, in the course of *this* scrutiny, we may find more that points us to Christ; for, as Nephi wrote,

2 Nephi 11:4   4 All things which have been given of God from the beginning of the world, unto man, are the typifying of him.

And, if such be the case, that all things that come from God are the typifying of Christ, we should be able to ponder over these familiar passages and see them in new light, in the brightness of he who is the Light of the World.

The End Time

To begin our reexamination we will go back in time. We will, for a few minutes, become one with the Savior's disciples near the end of his mortal ministry. For a moment in this oneness, we are on the temple grounds in Old Jerusalem. We walk with Jesus now as he meanders about. During this day he has uttered such offensive language as the Pharisees and scribes had never heard used to their faces. He has called these leaders of Jewish society hypocrites and snakes and murderers of prophets. The collective ire of Jerusalem's elite has been raised to levels impossible to measure. It is certain that they will act against this Galilean who has turned their world upside down. It is certain that Jesus knows what he has done. And now we watch as he walks about the temple grounds surveying the scene, knowing his own death is very near. The Lord's Apostles walk with him and show him the glory of the temple, the greatest landmark of the Holy City. Their gestures are a reflection of the awe that still accompanies each visit to the City of David. Seeing their admiration, the Lord provides them with a dose of eternal perspective. "See ye not all these things?" he asks, knowing full well that they see not only the building, but all of its accoutrements. "Verily I say unto you," he continues, "There shall not be left here one stone upon another, that shall not be thrown down" (Matthew 24:2).

These disciples are fishermen, not engineers, but they appreciate the quality workmanship and glorious symbolism of the sacred temple. For them the temple of Jerusalem is the ultimate symbol of the eternal existence of God. It is his house. It is his domain. The destruction of this magnificent edifice is an idea which cannot be conceived in their reality. Trusting that Jesus would not lie, they ask a simple question—when?

The Lord does not answer their question in *time*, speaking of hours or days or dates on a calendar. He answers with in terms of *events*. Jesus tells his disciples what to look for. That is to say, in the account that has come down to us from generations past, from the King James translators of the Holy Bible, we have recorded what Jesus said to his disciples, to his followers in his day. In that record, the Lord's answer is clearly addressed to the disciples of two millennia ago. "Take heed that no man deceive you," the Savior says (Matthew 24:4). And in the next several passages of sacred text the Lord reveals all that they, the ancient disciples, must do to avoid deception, assuring them that "this generation [the generation of the ancient Apostles] shall not pass, till all these things be fulfilled" (Matthew 24:34). The words are clear. We hear them speaking to *us*, but the events described in our treasured text are clearly intended for the narrower audience of the Savior's disciples of long ago. The translation that has to come to us from the Bible appears to be a message designed exclusively for people who lived two thousand years ago.

Through the miracle of Restoration scripture, an inspired revision has come to this generation—our generation. It is the Joseph Smith Translation of the Bible, which adds new clarity and focus to these events, all the events that Jesus spoke of at this time of reflection and sacred instruction. The Lord impressed upon the mind of the Prophet Joseph Smith the concept of *two* messages, not one, that came from the heart of the Son of God. In both the King James Version and the Joseph Smith Translation, we see Jesus and his associates walking east across the Kidron Valley to the Mount of Olives. It is there that the disciples ask the "when?" question. But it is evident that the answer given by the Son of God and restored through the Prophet Joseph has wider application than that given to those first century followers of the Savior. After describing the events that the ancient Apostles would witness for themselves, the Lord says:

JS—M 1:21

21 Behold, these things [the events pertaining to the generation in which the ancient Apostles lived] I have spoken unto you concerning the Jews; and again, *after* the tribulation of those days which shall come upon Jerusalem [after that generation has passed], if any man shall say unto you, Lo, here is Christ, or there, believe him not. [Emphasis added.]

Later, he is more emphatic in his effort to show that this message pertains to another group, a group that will succeed the holy Apostles in some future generation. "Behold," declares the Son of God, "I speak for mine elect's sake" (JS—M 1:29); the "very elect . . . according to the covenant" (JS—M 1:22).

Armed with this precious perspective, guided by this idea, it becomes apparent that at least half the message of Matthew 24, the message given to the ancient Apostles, pertains to and is addressed to those who will live in the generation when Christ comes in his glory to begin his millennial reign. Yet it is not addressed to *all* of that generation. It is addressed to the *very elect according to the covenant.* Through the Prophet's inspired revision we see a new audience receiving the Lord's revelation of the end time. We see the Saints of the Most High God, those who have given their all for the building up of his kingdom, those who have suffered humiliation and desolation for the testimony of Jesus, those who have received the new and everlasting covenant of the restored gospel of Jesus Christ, who have brought themselves under covenant and have tried with all their hearts to keep that covenant. We see Latter-day Saints of every age, ethnic background, and social strata, of every color and country, sprinkled as savoring salt in all their lands of promise. It is to them that the Lord's sequential unfolding of events is addressed. And here is that sequence, as it appears in the Prophet's inspired revision, together with the Lord's commentary.

1. False Christs shall come among the people, perhaps deceiving "the very elect, who are the elect according to the covenant" (JS—M 1:22).
2. There will be wars and rumors of wars. "See that ye be not troubled . . . the end is not yet" (JS—M 1:23).
3. Nations and kingdoms will rise up against one another.
4. Natural disasters of every kind will abound.
5. There will be an abundance of sin.
6. Coldness rather than love will prevail among the people of the earth. "He that shall not be overcome [by the absence of love], the same shall be saved" (JS—M 1:30).
7. The gospel of the kingdom will be preached in all the world. "And then shall the end come, or the destruction of the wicked" (JS—M 1:31).
8. The "abomination of desolation, spoken of by Daniel the prophet," will befall Jerusalem (JS—M 1:32). By this we understand that Jerusalem will come under siege *again*, as it did in the days of the Lord's Apostles.[1]
9. The sun and moon will be darkened and stars will fall from heaven. "This generation, in which these things shall be shown forth, shall not pass away until all I have told you shall be fulfilled" (JS—M 1:34).
10. "After the tribulation of those days, and the powers of the heavens shall be shaken, then shall appear the sign of the Son of Man in heaven . . . with power and great glory. . . . He shall send his angels before him with the great sound of the trumpet, and they shall gather together the remainder of his elect from the four winds, from one end of heaven to the other" (JS—M 1:36–37).

Preparation for the End Time

This is the unfolding, the modern revelation of the end times. While it may be of some comfort to know the nature of the events, to know what will happen, to know that there is ultimate hope for the future and for the faithful; still, there is that gnawing passage that eats away at our souls that troubling thought that the times will be so confusing, the wonders so convincing that "if possible, they shall deceive the very elect, who are the elect according to the covenant" (JS—M 1:22). To the minds of the faithful there comes the horrible question: How can the very elect be deceived? How is it possible? The scriptures remain silent on the matter. Nevertheless, the Lord does not leave his elect without any direction, principles, or doctrine. Directly to the elect he gives these precious gems:

JS—M 1:37, 39, 48   **37** Whoso treasureth up my word, shall not be deceived. . . .
39 Mine elect, when they shall see all these things, they shall know that he is near. . . .
48 Be ye also ready, for in such an hour as ye think not, the Son of Man cometh.

Furthermore, the Master provides several vignettes to help the elect see how obvious the Second Coming will be. For example: when you see eagles circling about in the sky, you know there is a dead body beneath them (see v. 27). The events leading up to the Second Coming of the Son of Man will be just as obvious in their meaning. In the days of Noah, the days of the great flood, people were marrying and living their lives normally "until the day that Noah entered into the ark" (v. 42). There will be no change in the day to day events of life. All will be normal to those who are not watching for the signs. If a man knew the night he would be robbed, "he would have watched" (see v. 47). In other words, there will be no preliminary announcements beyond the signs given to the elect. With these allegorical offerings to stiffen their resolve, the elect according to the covenant should come away with this assurance: the signs of the Second Coming will be obvious, and the only way to prepare is to watch at all times. There will be no signal, no whistle blowing, no beat of a drum to alert one and all that the promised day has at last arrived. It will come as naturally as the dawn follows the darkness.

There it is, the unfolding of the end time, the chronology, the warnings, the principles, everything except the exact date, which "no one knoweth;

no not the angels of God in heaven, but my Father only" (v. 40).

And yet there is more to come. The Lord has given his disciples a sense of what the end time will be like, what the events will be. But, to give his disciples greater understanding of how the events will unfold, he speaks to them in parables—three of them. They are the end time parables. The Joseph Smith Translation begins these parables with these sobering words: "And then, at that day, before the Son of Man comes, the kingdom of heaven shall be likened unto ten virgins" (JS—M 25:1). This inspired revision helps us see that there is a clear connection between the ideas presented in Matthew 24 and this current chapter. The three parables in Matthew 25 are thus transformed. No longer are they interesting anecdotes. They are messages to the elect according to the covenant, each one explaining some unique manner of preparation that must prevail when the elect stand before God to be judged. Prophetically, we should also see the Lord himself in these accounts, remembering that all that is given by God to man is "the typifying of [Christ]" (2 Nephi 11:4). In each parable we should be able to see him in ways that are obvious and in ways that are not so apparent.

The Parable of the Ten Virgins

As we read the parable of the ten virgins it seems natural to associate the bridegroom with the Savior. The idea of the Lord being the groom and the church or Israel being the bride has been promoted since Old Testament times. The evident problem with this spontaneous association, connecting the bridegroom with Christ, is that there is in this particular bridegroom no evidence of mercy. On the surface there is only roughness and disdain for those who are foolish. There is only justice. The wise are admitted to the wedding feast. The foolish are rejected. Where is evidence of grace? Where do we see that enabling power generated by the Atonement of Christ in this judgment scenario? Is it in the extra oil that the wise virgins refuse to share? If that is true, what could the extra oil represent? To our minds come the Savior's sobering warning:

JS—M 1:37   **37** Whoso treasureth up my word, shall not be deceived.

They that are wise treasure up the word of God and the knowledge that they possess is not something that can be shared. It comes from daily feasting upon the Word in such a way that a oneness with the Word is achieved. Such a treasure cannot be shared because it is gained only from experience. Can a mother tell her daughter what it is like to give birth and hope to have the daughter understand? Can a father tell a son what it is like to give a priesthood blessing to a sick person and truly convey all that such an experience represents? Surely not!

The wise virgins treasure their extra oil. They will not be separated from it. They do not know the exact time when the groom will arrive. They only know that all the signs have been given to signal the day; and it is dark, very dark. They will need their lamps. They will need to treasure the word of God.

Notwithstanding the apparent lack of mercy in this parable, there is a typifying of Christ and his mercy. It is in the *invitation*, the implicit invitation to come to the wedding. All have lamps, all are virgins, all have been invited. They have everything they need to participate in the wedding feast. So too we may say that through the Atonement we have been given all that we need to stand before God at the great day of the Lord to account for our lives. Passages of Restoration scripture that employ wedding feast euphemisms confirm that the elect according to the covenant have received all that is needed to be ready. In each case, these references consist of invitations to come to Christ, to come to his kingdom. "Prepare ye the way of the Lord," shout the thousands who march in advance of his coming in the generation of his arrival.

D&C 65:3	3 Prepare ye the supper of the Lamb, make ready for the Bridegroom.

And, to those who have accepted the invitation, to those who, by baptism and receiving of the Holy Ghost by the laying on of hands, have been gathered into his kingdom, the Lord cries out,

D&C 33:17–18	17 Be faithful, praying always, having your lamps trimmed and burning, and oil with you, that you may be ready at the coming of the Bridegroom— 18 For behold, verily, verily, I say unto you, that I come quickly.

And in that day when the Lord comes again,

D&C 45:57	57 They that are wise and have received the truth, and have taken the Holy Spirit for their

> guide, and have not been deceived . . . shall
> abide the day.

Without the Atonement there is no invitation. There is no point to preparation. There is no reason to repent, to have faith, to have a lamp or extra oil. The virgins have been told to gather. Evidence of the arrival of the groom has been given. They must abide the day. The grace of God is seen in the invitation. This is a message to the elect, not to the whole world. It is to the very elect who may be deceived. Through the gift of the Atonement of Christ we may access all the gifts and blessings that await the faithful. However, the parable makes it clear that those who are invited must abide the day. They must be ready, treasuring up the word of God, taking the Holy Spirit for their guide, receiving the truth. Were those in this parable of a wide variety of people, old men, toddlers, mothers and sons, we would look at it differently. Because they are all virgins, a unique subset of a culture, we see them as the personification of a unique subset of God's children. We see them as the elect according to the covenant. Half were wise. Half were foolish. Can we expect it will be otherwise for the elect when the end time comes?

Who are the *wise* of our own generation? My father is such a man. Remember, one of the characteristics of the modern elect is that they have taken the Holy Spirit for their guide. I recall a scene many years ago in which I was sitting on a park bench in the dead of winter with my father. We were watching children at play: my grandchildren, his great-grandchildren. We sat huddled in winter parkas looking straight ahead, hoping to stay warm. From out of nowhere, my father said, "I think there may have been a time, when you were about sixteen years old, when I may have looked at you in a way that might have suggested I didn't love you. I want you to know how sorry I am." Thirty-five years after the event that troubled his soul, my father felt a prompting from the Holy Spirit, took that prompting as a guide, and tried to make things right. For my part, I could not remember such a moment and told him so. He patted my knee and we resumed our watch. From this and other similar experiences I have concluded that my father will have made things right with the God he loves before the Bridegroom comes.

There are also examples of those who are not prepared or preparing. One who had not prepared, who had not taken the Holy Spirit for her guide, who had not accepted the invitation extended through the Atonement, was a friend who, when her father died, exclaimed, "I can never forgive God for taking my dad, never!" What this woman, who has so many other good qualities, was saying is "I can never forgive God for taking my dad on *his* timetable rather than *mine*." The soul of my friend, the vessel of oil, was devoid of the spiritual power that is necessary to survive life's crises. It was evident then. It has proven to be evident since.

In these examples, the essence of the response to life's challenges by those who are prepared is love, love of God and all mankind (see 2 Nephi 31:20). I noticed this as a mission president. The longer I associated with the missionaries, the more often I went out teaching with them, the longer I poured over the scriptures and the doctrine, the more inclined I was to tell the missionaries that I loved them. In fact, the more inclined I was to tell everyone of my love for them. It is the natural outgrowth of understanding and accepting the Atonement.

If we are wise, we will not stop reading at the end of the parable of the ten virgins. We will continue, seeing this parable as part of a trilogy of tests that will be given to the elect in the day when the Lord comes again. Lesson number one is to take advantage of the Atonement and use it to prepare in such a way that we will not be deceived. What of lessons two and three?

The Parable of the Talents

The second test is illustrated in the parable of the talents. While much has been written concerning the deeper meaning and intent of this parable, we will confine our examination to those statements that appear in scripture.

A master determines to go to a far country, a distant location. The privilege given to his trusted associates is to become his servants. "A man . . . called his own servants, and delivered unto them his goods" (Matthew 25:14). Notice the careful wording—not just servants, not just his servants—his *own* servants. The wording awakens us: if we remember the connection between the prophecies in Matthew 24, we must conclude that these servants are once again a typifying of the very elect, the elect according to the covenant. They are not everyone's servants. They are unique. They are the servants of the Lord. They are set apart from the rest of the world, different, his own.

They are given stewardships to watch over. They are given talents. We suppose that, in the context of the scripture account, these talents are sums of money. A talent, as the term is used in the parable, is a certain weight of silver or gold. Traditionally, the value of a talent of gold or silver has been established at nearly 76 pounds of these precious metals.[2] In an effort to give the parable more modern relevance we will calculate the value of a talent using today's gold standard. Let us assume that the current value of gold is approximately $625 per ounce. The value of a pound of gold would be $10,000. So, the value of a talent of gold (76 pounds) would be $760,000. Thus, the value of five talents, the stewardship given to the first servant, would be $3,800,000. The servant who received two talents would have as his stewardship $1,520,000; and obviously, the servant who received one talent of gold would acquire $760,000. These sums, even in an inflationary era, seem overwhelming in their size. So too, the precious gift of the Atonement is beyond calculation. It is God's investment in us. "The worth of souls is great in the sight of God," we are assured by the Lamb of God (D&C 18:10).

D&C 18:11

11 For, behold, the Lord your Redeemer suffered death in the flesh; wherefore he suffered the pain of all men, that all men might repent and come unto him. And he hath risen again from the dead, that he might bring all men unto him, on conditions of repentance.

Our worth is defined by the cost paid for our redemption. The Lord gave all that he had. Therefore the cost, that is to say the worth of our souls, is incalculable.

Remember, these servants are not just any servants. They are the servants of the Lord—his own. They receive these sums of money *according to their ability* (see Matthew 25:15). The stewardships have been calculated by the master to be equivalent to the capacities of the recipients. There is no chance for injustice. The test is fair. Therefore, the judgment given when the master returns from his long journey will be equally fair. When the judgment scenario is played out, the question will not be: Who acquired the most? It will be: What did you do with what the master gave you? What did you do with the gifts God gave you that were calculated to be *consistent with your abilities*? Or, boiling the question down to its simplest expression: What did you do with the gifts God alone could give you?

Two servants double the investment the Lord made in them. Notwithstanding the great difference in the final tally, those who doubled their master's investment received equivalent rewards. First, the acknowledgement that they had done well: "Well done, thou good and faithful servant," followed by a reward for faithfulness: "Thou hast been faithful over a few things, I will make thee ruler over many things: enter thou into the joy of thy lord" (Matthew 25:21, 23).

One servant did nothing with his stewardship. His "reward" was a scathing rebuke and the loss of all that he had been given. Remember, this is what the kingdom of heaven will be like, the judgment moment, the end time, the final accounting. And it will be the accounting given to the Lord's elect, the elect according to the covenant. What are the talents that the Lord has given to the elect? Modern revelation gives us a divine perspective.

First, *authority to preach the gospel of repentance.* The Lord declared,

D&C 60:2–3   **2** With some I am not well pleased, for they will not open their mouths, but they hide *the talent which I have given unto them* because of the fear of man. . . .
3 If they are not more faithful unto me, it shall be taken away, even that which they have. [Emphasis added.]

Second, *time.* In the ancient parable, the unprofitable servant buried his talent in the earth. The modern equivalent to burying our talents is, according to the Lord, wasting time.

D&C 60:13   **13** Thou shalt not idle away thy time, neither shalt thou *bury thy talent* that it shall not be known. [Emphasis added.]

Third, *the law of consecration.* This law was given:

D&C 82:18–19   **18** . . . for the benefit of the church of the living God, that every man may *improve upon his talent*, that every man may gain other talents, yea, even an hundred fold, to be cast into the Lord's storehouse, to become the common property of the whole church—
19 Every man seeking the interest of his neighbor, and doing all things with an eye single to the glory of God. [Emphasis added.]

These three gifts—the gospel, time to preach it, and a law to apply it—are the only blessings connected to the parable of the talents in Restoration scripture.

Based upon the Lord's revealed word, what must be done to pass the second test, to multiply talents, spiritually speaking? We must use our time in proclaiming the gospel, in consecrating all that we have and are to the building up of the Church and the building up of our neighbors, with an eye single to the glory of God. The pattern of the Lord's disciples when they know their sins have been remitted is best described in the writings of Enos. The redeemed, like Enos, seek forgiveness. Then, once that forgiveness has been achieved, motivated by the joy they have experienced and the love they feel from God and for him, they pour out their hearts for their family and eventually for all mankind (see Enos 1:4–11).

There are those who bury their talents. I remember one missionary with whom I served, a bright young man. He would not go tracting or engage in missionary service of any kind from about 10 AM to 5 PM. He was the most gifted teacher in the mission. This young man could quote the scriptures easily and used them brilliantly in the presentation of his lessons. When I discovered that he was not taking advantage of the time the Lord had given him, I went to his apartment, as his mission president, to offer counsel. The apartment was a mess. It was cluttered with books: Church history, Church doctrine, commentaries. When I presented the problem, that he was not working as he should, he explained that tracting was the least effective of all forms of missionary work. "There is something that is less effective," I said.

"What's that?"

"Sitting in your apartment all day."

A missionary who would squander this precious time, this precious gift to proclaim the gospel, neither understands nor appreciates the gift of the Atonement. After reviewing that doctrine the elder made a commitment to use the *talent* the Lord had given him, and he lived true to his word.

I compare this unfortunate example with another missionary who did seem to appreciate the gifts he had been given. One summer afternoon I arranged to meet this elder at his apartment. The purpose of my visit was to tell him that his mother had unexpectedly passed away. He was of course stunned. While she had been sickly for some time, it was expected that she would be able to survive well past the time of his return from the mission field. Tears filled his eyes as he spoke of his dear mother. After a time, he was silent. Then a smile came over his countenance. I asked what he was thinking. "She'll be able to see me now," he said. "She'll be able to see what I'm doing and not just read about it in my letters." This young man's service became a monument, a tribute to a faithful mother. In the larger sense, it became a tribute to God, who had given him time to show gratitude for a gospel this elder so clearly understood.

So far, we have seen in the two end time parables, elements essential to exaltation, gifts that can only come from God through the Atonement of his Son, two blessings without which eternal life is not possible: the invitation to come to Christ's kingdom (the invitation to the wedding feast), and the resources (talents) to invite others to join with and become part of the elect according to the covenant.

The Parable of the Sheep and the Goats

The third and final parable is the culmination of the final judgment scenario. We will assume that the elect according to the covenant have passed the first two tests. They have been baptized, received the Holy Ghost, and received the resources and time whereby they might bring others to Christ. They have not been deceived and they have used their resources wisely. What can remain?

In the final parable of this trilogy—the sheep and the goats—the sheep are gathered on the right hand of the king, the goats on the left. Implicit in this scene is the idea that the sheep and goats have previously been mixed together. It is the whole world that is gathered before the king. The elect according to the covenant will be mixed in with all mankind. Those who are like sheep will be gathered to one place; those who are like goats, to another. To the meek, the compliant, the willing, the ones who will be comfortable with and have been redeemed by the Lamb of God, the invitation will be to gather on the right hand of the Redeemer. They will be invited to sit at his right-hand, as he sits on the right hand of the Father.

To the stubborn, the whiners, the rebellious, the goats of this world, there will be a place provided on the left, where there will be no glory. The placing on the right and left hand is judgment. In this parable the elect are not waiting for the arrival of the Bridegroom. They have already demonstrated that they cannot be deceived. They have received no assignments from the Master. They have already demonstrated that they will magnify that which the Lord has given them. In this scenario the judgment is rendered. It is a *fait accompli*. There is nothing to say, no appeal, no second chance. It is done.

There seems to be a peculiar irony as we discover how it is that those on the right hand merited such noble positioning. What did they do to justify this reward from the king? They helped the poor and the needy, and in so doing, they seem oblivious to the fact that such service was the great requirement for admittance to this place of honor. They are surprised. They demand to know, "When saw we thee an hungered and fed thee?"

If they are caught off guard, and it is evident that they are, why did they render such service? What was their motivation for helping the poor? On this matter the parable is silent, but the scriptures are not. "Are we not all beggars?" asks King Benjamin to the people of Zarahemla. "Do we not all depend upon the same Being, even God, for all the substance we have?" (Mosiah 4:19).

What is the motivation?

We are all helpless and have received all that we need from God. Through the Savior's precious Atonement we have received the resurrection. We have also received remission of sins on conditions of repentance. Can we resurrect ourselves? Can we forgive our own sins so as to merit admission into the kingdom of God? Surely we cannot!

We ought to show our gratitude by helping others. Such is the thinking of those who will "inherit the kingdom prepared for [them] from the foundation of the world" (Matthew 25:34). Thus, what is the final element of redemption that is given to the elect according to the covenant? What else do they need beyond the gospel, beyond time and resources to proclaim the gospel, beyond the law of consecration? It is the poor and needy! Without the poor and needy of the earth the elect have no vehicle to overcome the natural tendency toward pride. Without the poor the elect cannot demonstrate selflessness, sacrifice, humility, and all other virtues that are called Christian—or Christlike. Without the poor, there is no redemption.

A dear sister in a stake I lived in years ago organized an effort to help the poor. It was astounding in its vastness and complexity. The program included regular visits to homeless shelters and soup kitchens and places where the poor were present in abundance. Ward members bristled because the project came as an assignment, much the same way other redemptive acts begin. Nobody asked them if they wanted to do this community service. It was presented as a duty, and it had to be fulfilled. So, by virtue of a feeling of consecration, ward members filled their assignment. We went and served the poor, in a variety of ways. We did not wonder as to how the poor arrived at their station. We went by assignment.

Over time, the most amazing thing happened. Fast offerings increased substantially and steadily. During the years that stake members participated in this mandatory compassion experience, their true compassion for the poor expanded dramatically. Their motivation became pure. Their desire became selfless. And, we have no doubt that the selfless organizer, who was faced with rebellion and near mutiny for her earthly reward during the early days of the project, will hear the King say, "Well done thou good and faithful servant."

Along with an understanding of the Lord's judgment, we have seen examples of an astounding progression in this examination of the end time parables. We have seen how the elect according to the covenant take advantage of the Atonement of Christ, how they avail themselves of the enabling power that can come only from the Son of God. *Guests* at a wedding feast (in the parable of the ten virgins) become *servants* (in the parable of the talents) who eventually *rule* over kingdoms (in the parable of the sheep and the goats). Similarly, we see the Son of God moving allegorically from *Bridegroom* (in the parable of the ten virgins) to *Master* (in the parable of the talents) to *King* (in the parable of the sheep and the goats). In fact, the Bridegroom becomes the King of Kings. The elect according to the covenant, become rulers over kingdoms if they are not deceived. And what is it that they must do to avoid deception?

- Accept the invitation to come to Christ. Watch and be ready, especially as the night of spiritual darkness grows closer to midnight. (The message of the parable of the ten virgins.)
- Magnify the investment the Lord has made in them. Use time wisely. Proclaim the gospel. Consecrate that which they are called upon to give to the building up of God's kingdom on the earth. (The message of the parable of the talents.)
- Look upon the poor and needy as their salvation. (The message of the parable of the sheep and the goats)

When the parable of the ten virgins is returned to its rightful place, to a position of counsel to those who are the Lord's elect, the elect according to the covenant, it is evident why Nephi would share with us his desire for his generation, for he saw things as they really are. He wrote,

2 Nephi 25:23   23 We labor diligently to write, to persuade
                          our children, and also our brethren, to believe

in Christ, and to be reconciled to God; for we
know that it is by grace that we are saved, after
all we can do.

It is abundantly clear that the grace and mercy extended to us by the
Lord is of no value unless we take advantage of that mercy by our actions.
We must accept the invitation, use the resources given to us, and care for
the poor. These are actions, and they are actions that matter.

Those who will not be deceived in the time before Jesus Christ comes
again will demonstrate a complete acceptance of his atoning sacrifice.
They will accept the invitation extended to them. They will come to the
wedding feast, and they will not lose faith by believing that the Savior
is "delaying his return." They will not squander the gifts God has given
them but will believe it is better to be anxiously engaged, rather than sit
on the sidelines during the unfolding events of the last days. They will
multiply the investment the Lord has made in them. They will see in the
poor and the needy the face of Christ and serve in meekness. They will
see in the face of the poor and needy the redemption that was given by
he who was "a man of sorrows and acquainted with grief," by he who
"was wounded for our transgressions" and "bruised for our iniquities"
by that Being who "was oppressed and afflicted," who was taken "from
prison and from judgment" (see Isaiah 53:3–8). They will watch and be
ready—to serve their fellow beings. For therein lies redemption through
the Atonement of Christ.

Notes
1. See Bible Dictionary, "abomination of desolation," 601.
2. See Bible Dictionary, "weights and measures," 789.

THE GOOD SAMARITAN

by Craig Frogley

In viewing this parable from an LDS perspective, several topics will be explored and juxtaposed against sectarian doctrines of salvation and life's practical realities. The focal point will be how the parable teaches us obvious as well as subtle doctrines concerning how to gain eternal life, as was asked by the lawyer in prompting the parable. Traditionally this parable is interpreted to teach the importance of service to those in need. Placing this important part of the gospel into context, both ancient and modern, will broaden the perspective of its place in so central a gospel teaching as the Atonement. We all seek to understand the Atonement but really need better understanding of how to apply it in our lives, including both its redemptive and enabling powers. The parable, as well as the chapter context into which it is embedded, furnishes wonderful insights that will aid us in this quest.

Luke 10:36–37	36 Which now of these three, thinkest thou, was neighbour unto him that fell among the thieves? 37 And he said, He that shewed mercy on him. Then said Jesus unto him, Go, and do thou likewise.

It would seem from the Savior's interrogatory, then, that I am neighbor unto those I show mercy. If so, then if I am to go and do likewise, I should be showing mercy unto everyone, thereby making them my neighbor. The context as given in verse 36 seems to point to the Savior's intent of contrasting the behavior of the three principle characters of the parable:

the priest, the Levite, and the Samaritan. Yet, ancient tradition[1] increases the application to include the fallen Jew, the robbers, and the innkeeper. According to these ancient texts, each character personified Adam, who suffered the wounds of the Fall through transgression; the law; the prophets; the Messiah; and finally, the disciples.

The parable is sufficiently intricate that many writers have designated it as an allegory where all of the elements are meant as metaphors strung together into a story that represents the path to eternal life. The elders in the meridian of time understood the story of the parable as one of "a certain man" (Adam) who descends from the holy city going both down and east, symbolizing leaving the presence of God, or the Fall. While on the road he succumbs to the dangers of mortality and is robbed and beaten and left to die (consequence of the Fall). The "certain priest" (the Law) and the Levite (the prophets) cannot save him. He is attended to by the Samaritan (the Messiah) who washes, anoints, and clothes him (ordinances of salvation) and takes him to the inn (the church) for care by the innkeeper (church leader, disciples) to whom he pays two denarii (the price of redemption paid yearly as a temple tax) with the charge to care for him, even if it costs more, and then he promises to return (the Second Coming).[2]

Among several clear applications was that the solution to the fallen state of man was not to be found in the law or the prophets. The law was important, as were the priest and Levite as administrators of essential ordinances tied to the Jewish temple. But their capacity to fill their formal calling would have been compromised by stopping to help their fallen countryman. (This will be discussed in greater detail later.) It, like them, could not save the fallen man.

It would be natural to assume that the law symbolized is the law of Moses as in Paul's statements in the following scriptures:

Romans 3:20, 28	**20** Therefore by the deeds of the law there shall no flesh be justified in his sight: for by the law is the knowledge of sin. **28** Therefore we conclude that a man is justified by faith without the deeds of the law.
Galatians 2:16	**16** Knowing that a man is not justified by the works of the law, but by the faith of Jesus Christ, even we have believed in Jesus Christ, that we

might be justified by the faith of Christ, and not by the works of the law: for by the works of the law shall no flesh be justified.

Galatians 3:11, 24

11 But that no man is justified by the law in the sight of God, it is evident: for, the just shall live by faith. . . .
24 Wherefore the law was our schoolmaster to bring us unto Christ, that we might be justified by faith.

Luke's statement clarifies that the law of Moses was the issue to these early missionaries and converts:

Acts 13:39

39 And by him all that believe are justified from all things, from which ye could not be justified by the law of Moses.

This would limit application of the principles in this parable, of our interaction with law, to the time of Christ, making it apply only as a message about the end of the law of Moses. But then James, the apparent half-brother of Jesus, uses the same verbiage as Paul, although he is clearly speaking of works of a different law through which justification comes:

James 2:21–24

21 Was not Abraham our father justified by works, when he had offered Isaac his son upon the altar?
22 Seest thou how faith wrought with his works, and by works was faith made perfect?
23 And the scripture was fulfilled which saith, Abraham believed God, and it was imputed unto him for righteousness: and he was called the Friend of God.
24 Ye see then how that by works a man is justified, and not by faith only.

Father Lehi further explains and complicates this interaction with law by expanding its definition:

2 Nephi 2:5

5 And men are instructed sufficiently that they know good from evil. And the law is given unto men. And by the law no flesh is justified; or, by the law men are cut off. Yea, by the temporal law they were cut off; and also, by the spiritual

> law they perish from that which is good, and
> become miserable forever.

If both the spiritual and natural laws condemn men, justification wouldn't come by law, yet apparently, according to James, it is obedience to law and its interaction with faith that must bring justification. This is confirmed in D&C 88:

D&C 88:34–35, 39 **34** And again, verily I say unto you, that which is governed by law is also preserved by law and perfected and sanctified by the same.
35 That which breaketh a law, and abideth not by law, but seeketh to become a law unto itself, and willeth to abide in sin, and altogether abideth in sin, cannot be sanctified by law, neither by mercy, justice, nor judgment. Therefore, they must remain filthy still. . . .
39 All beings who abide not in those conditions are not justified.

As used here, *perfected* (v. 34) is synonymous with *justified* (v. 39) and with Lehi's use of justified. *Perfected* here cannot mean *sanctified*, since verse 34 explains that perfection *and* sanctification come through law. Lehi said that the law wouldn't justify, but that doesn't mean that it couldn't, for in verse 7 he goes on to say that Christ answered both ends of the law: to perfect and to condemn. Christ was perfected or justified by the law. So Lehi says that man who isn't justified by law must be redeemed by Christ (v. 6). Since D&C 88 made it clear that both sanctification and justification, or perfection, come by obedience to the law, redemption must somehow employ law through Christ.

This is where sectarian doctrine sometimes attempts to solve the puzzle. It teaches that justification, the legal declaration of innocence, comes through redemption by accepting Christ, who then justifies your sins with his suffering. In short, the Atonement delivers man from justice, or the condemnation for disobedience to law. Elder McConkie comments,

> What is lacking in the sectarian world is a true knowledge of the law of justification. Simply stated that law is this: " 'All covenants, contracts, bonds, obligations, oaths, vows, performances, connections, associations, or expectations' (D&C 132:7), in which men must abide to be saved and exalted, must be entered into and performed in righteousness so that the Holy Spirit can justify the candidate for salvation

in what has been done" (see 1 Nephi 16:2; Jacob 2:13–14; Alma 41:15; D&C 98; 132:1, 62). An act that is justified by the Spirit is one that is sealed by the Holy Spirit of Promise, or in other words, ratified and approved by the Holy Ghost. This law of justification is the provision the Lord has placed in the gospel to assure that no unrighteous performance will be binding on earth and in heaven, and that no person will add to his position or glory in the hereafter by gaining an unearned blessing.

"As with all other doctrines of salvation, justification is available because of the atoning sacrifice of Christ, but it becomes operative in the life of an individual only on conditions of personal righteousness. As Paul taught, men are not justified by the works of the Mosaic Law alone any more than men are saved by those works alone. The grace of God, manifest through the infinite and eternal atonement wrought by his Son, makes justification a living reality for those who seek righteousness (see Isaiah 53:11; Mosiah 14:11)" (McConkie, *Mormon Doctrine*, 408).[3]

President Harold B. Lee corroborates this explanation:

I want to comment about this one statement: "by the Spirit ye are justified" (Moses 6:60). Now I've struggled with that statement, and I have found a definition that seems to indicate to me what I'm sure the Lord intended to convey. The definition that I think is significant says: "Justify means to pronounce free from guilt or blame, or to absolve." Now if the Spirit, the Holy Ghost, is to pronounce one free from guilt or blame, or to absolve, then we begin to see something of the office of the Holy Ghost that relates to the subject about which we are talking: what it means to be born of the Spirit.

I shall inject here another phrase that is oft discussed (and I think is misunderstood) and to which we try to attach some mysteries. This phrase, where the Lord directs that all of these things are to be eternal, is: "must be sealed by the Holy Spirit of promise." Let me refer first to the 76th section of the Doctrine and Covenants. Speaking of those who are candidates for celestial glory, the Lord says:

". . . by keeping the commandments they might be washed and cleansed from all their sins. . . . And who overcome by faith, and are sealed by the Holy Spirit of Promise, which the Father sheds forth upon all those who are just and true" (D&C 76:51–53).[4]

Understanding the synergy between works (as obedience to law), faith, and grace helps clarify how the Atonement delivers us both from and to justice and is the genius of the parable. In the Joseph Smith Translation of Paul we find:

JST, Romans 4:16

16 Therefore ye are justified of faith and works, through grace, to the end the promise might be sure to all the seed; not to them only who are of the law, but to them also who are of the faith of Abraham; who is the father of us all.

In context, *law*, in verses 34 and 39 of D&C 88, referring to being justified and sanctified by law, points us again to Christ, but this time as the force that governs all creation and originates in him as the Light of Christ.

D&C 88:12–13

12 Which light proceedeth forth from the presence of God to fill the immensity of space—
13 The light which is in all things, which giveth life to all things, which is the law by which all things are governed, even the power of God who sitteth upon his throne, who is in the bosom of eternity, who is in the midst of all things.

The seeming paradox relating to law or works will make more sense in view of two definitions of law from *Encyclopedia of Mormonism*:

Descriptive Law: "The divine law that operates directly upon or through physical and biological orders."[5]

This seems to describe the operational physics of the universe. This natural law by which all things work, called the Light of Christ in section 88, either dictates how things can be ordered and perfected or, by disobedience, destroyed. This is comparable to a recipe by which a perfect cake can be baked. Father Lehi isn't telling us that the recipe doesn't work but rather that men can't follow the recipe alone. We need help lest the spoiled cake be allowed to define our failure and end our progression. Metaphorically, of course, it isn't the cake but what we become that defines the success or failure.

Any set of parents, wanting to be responsible and preserve the life of their child, might clearly state natural law by instructing their toddler to not play on the very busy road passing in front of their house. "Don't go into the road because you will be killed." But they would instinctively know that stating the natural law wouldn't save the child. This natural physics of God's universe can also be called his justice. Again note some definitions:

In Hebrew, the language of the Old Testament, the word *justice* is *Tsdaqah*, which means righteousness, or the capacity to make a covenant and always keep it. Justice is God's capacity to always do what he says he will do.

Moses 4:30

> 30 For as I, the Lord God, liveth, even so my words cannot return void, for as they go forth out of my mouth they must be fulfilled.

It is "God's justice." Were it not so, man could not have faith in him. Though we say that we prefer mercy over justice, it is God's justice that enables us to have faith in him or place our trust in him. God's justice perfects man. The natural laws that result from the physics of his divine light in and through all things, either serve to perfect or destroy, depending on whether the Creation remains consistent in behavior with this law. But due to the veil man doesn't remain consistent with it and so is condemned by it. The cake is spoiled; the toddler would be killed.

Understanding that justice is God always doing what he says he will do, allows us to understand that it isn't that God is subject to some outside code of laws. He is self-existent and, like truth, he abides. He would cease to be God if he didn't follow through because no one could have faith in a changeable or capricious god.

Mosiah 15:27

> 27 Therefore ought ye not to tremble? For salvation cometh to none such; for the Lord hath redeemed none such; yea, neither can the Lord redeem such; for he cannot deny himself; for he cannot deny justice when it has its claim.

Justice is God; it is "himself." Justice is one of God's attributes:

The justice of God: "Justice is not just an abstract principle, not merely some eternal ideal, some mystical regulation in a law-driven universe. Justice is an attribute of Deity, a condition and requirement of God. It is the justice *of God* which rewards righteousness. It is the justice *of God* which punishes sin."[6]

But if this attribute—justice—or the physics of the universe through the Light of Christ cannot save man (though it could if man were capable of full obedience), how is he saved? There is another attribute and type of law that makes sense of this seeming riddle:

Prescriptive Law: "Other laws of God are prescriptive. They address the free will of man, setting forth standards and rules of behavior necessary for salvation and for social harmony."[7]

This set of laws, like a prescription written by a doctor, is custom made for the various circumstances of man's mortality. These laws aren't necessarily inherent in the nature of things or even directly connected to the physics of the universe.

Alma 42:22

22 But there is a law given, and a punishment affixed, and a repentance granted; which repentance, mercy claimeth; otherwise, justice claimeth the creature and executeth the law, and the law inflicteth the punishment; if not so, the works of justice would be destroyed, and God would cease to be God.

Here the law is "given" (rather than naturally occurring) and the punishment is "affixed" (rather than being inherent). To continue with the toddler metaphor, these laws result from parental love and knowledge of both the circumstances and the person. The parent might say to the toddler, "So that you won't get hurt I will close the gate to the fence. It will protect you." Or, "If you go near the road you will have to stay in the house." These are transient laws to which a "punishment is affixed" (Alma 42:17, 22). These laws are an outgrowth of God's mercy.

Perhaps this may serve to bring metaphorical correspondence to the need for two characters in the parable representing that which cannot save, the "certain priest" and "the Levite." Lehi, Paul, and James all taught that man is not saved by law alone, to which we might add: prescriptive or descriptive law. The parable furnishes the key element in salvation and some processes by which salvation is promised.

But a deeper understanding of God's mercy is needed to show "how to come unto him to be saved" (1 Nephi 15:14). Mercy is usually understood to be compassion, but a search again of the original linguistic intent enlarges that understanding. In Hebrew there are five words and their derivatives that are translated as *mercy*. Compassion is its translation only a few times. Over 97 percent of the time the translation comes from two Hebrew words: *checed* or *raham* (or a derivative).

Checed literally refers to the love between two seasoned spouses. Christ chastised the law-quoting Pharisees by referring to Hosea 6:6. Here the Lord compares his desire for deep relationship with Israel to

Hosea and his wife. He contrasts that desire to the sacrifice that had been intended to produce love but instead had been ritualized, even trivialized by inexpensive offerings (see Matt 9:13). *Checed* is the word from which *mercy* is translated, rendering God's desire one of a loving relationship rather than mercy.

Hosea 6:6
6 For I desired mercy and not sacrifice, and the knowledge of God more than burnt offerings.

Raham refers to the love a mother has for her children. Its roots come from the word *womb* as in this verse:

2 Samuel 24:14
14 Let us fall now into the hand of the Lord; for his mercies are great: and let me not fall into the hand of man.

This is the love that brings a mother to self-sacrifice in order to save her young. Together these two words describe the contextual meaning of God's mercy. Alma quoted Zenos in explaining how little we understand it:

Alma 33:16
16 For behold, he said: Thou art angry, O Lord, with this people, because they will not understand thy mercies which thou hast bestowed upon them because of thy Son.

Isaiah seems to use hyperbole (though it is more likely divine reality) in comparison-contrast to explain this concept to his listeners. Note, for example, the oft-quoted scripture used to show God's greatness:

Isaiah 55:8–9
8 For my thoughts are not your thoughts, neither are your ways my ways, saith the Lord.
9 For as the heavens are higher than the earth, so are my ways higher than your ways, and my thoughts than your thoughts.

To contemplate the difference between our ways and his would be like considering the distance from earth to the heavens. One little four-year-old asked her daddy, "Can you touch the sky?"

"No," he said sadly.

"Yes you can, Daddy, try!"

He reached up and said, "See, daddies can't touch the sky."

"You aren't really trying, Daddy. Try harder!" He jumped, causing his fingers to hit the ceiling.

"There," she said triumphantly, "I told you that you could touch the sky!"

To a four-year-old the sky was the ceiling. Sometimes we have that same perspective when reading this verse. How high are the heavens above the earth? What is even more amazing than this seeming infinity is finding the context of the ways and thoughts God is talking about. Note verse 7, the one just before the one we have all heard.

Isaiah 55:7   7 Let the wicked forsake his way, and the unrighteous man his thoughts: and let him return unto the Lord, and he will have mercy upon him; and to our God, for he will abundantly pardon.

He is speaking about his mercy being above anything we could even consider. Except that he isn't just talking about being nice. He is talking about his love. He uses these Hebrew roots together in Psalms:

Psalm 51:1   1 Have mercy [*chanan*] upon me, O God, according to thy lovingkindness [*checed*]: according unto the multitude of thy tender mercies [*raham*] blot out my transgressions.

Like two different sides of a coin, mercy and justice cannot be separated when speaking of the attributes of God. Notice how they are used together here:

D&C 97:2   2 I, the Lord, show mercy unto all the meek, and upon all whomsoever I will, that I may be justified when I shall bring them unto judgment.

Here he cannot be just or justified unless he shows mercy. This pattern of relationship is amplified in Hebrew law. According to James E. Talmage, the courts could not judge someone guilty unanimously. There needed to be someone on the court that took their side in order for justice to be fully rendered. "By a provision that must appear to us most unusual, if all the judges voted for conviction on a capital charge the verdict was not to stand and the accused had to be set at liberty; for, it was argued, a unanimous vote against a prisoner indicated that he had had no friend or defender in court, and that the judges might have been in conspiracy against Him."[8]

Both mercy and justice are his attributes. Elder Packer noted that we will learn "that Justice is another name for Mercy, and Mercy is another name for Justice."[9]

Hence mercy, through prescribed law and its corrective punishments and rewards, schools us until we are capacitated, through grace and "all we can do," to live the full law consistent with God's justice, or as Elder McConkie used it, to be justified. Again, mercy delivers us both from and to justice. While the descriptive law used alone would cause our destruction, the prescriptive law would bring punishment or correction but not destruction. We then are redeemed from descriptive law and allowed to struggle with the prescriptive laws during a probationary time of mortality. During this time the key element, the enabling power of the Atonement (or grace), gradually capacitates our obedience to descriptive law until we receive "a fullness," hence becoming perfected or justified by law. Thus the interaction of mercy and justice through the redemptive and enabling power or grace of the Atonement reconcile Father Lehi with Joseph Smith and help us see the power of the parable of the good Samaritan.

Salvation from the fallen state in the parable of the Samaritan came through the process of a joint partnership that included: (1) *the Samaritan:* one that was hated and scorned as prophesied in Isaiah 53 (Ironically, salvation as personified in the Samaritan represented Christ who was telling the parable in response to scorn by a challenging lawyer seeking to tempt him and then justify himself [see Luke 10:25, 29].), and (2) *the innkeeper,* through delegation (representing those who are called to lead or manage the affairs of the Church). Here the Messiah invites three things:

1. The use of our talents and resources already in our possession or bestowed at the time of the call.
2. The sacrifice of that which we have earned to care for those brought to our circle of influence.
3. Faith in his promise to repay at some future time.

Both the Jew and the innkeeper are saved, one by redemption, the other by obedience and service.

The invitation to joint saviorship defines how we "go and do likewise," thereby becoming joint heirs with one whose mercy is then not just compassionate but also capacitating.

This certainly seems grander in scope than the expected answer to the lawyer's question, "Who is my neighbor?" But a closer look, using Joseph

Smith's invitation to examine the question that sparked the telling of the parable leads us to see that the original question was "What do I do to inherit eternal life?" In light of John's statement concerning Christ and the process by which he inherited eternal life, this parable takes on greater weight in the library of parables. Note:

D&C 93:12–13   12 And I, John, saw that he received not of the fullness at the first, but received grace for grace;
13 *And he received not of the fullness at first, but continued from grace to grace, until he received a fullness.* [Emphasis added.]

So he received grace as he gave grace and then continued from one level of divine investiture to a higher one until fullness of capacity and its resultant endowment ensued. This is further detailed by adding verse 19:

D&C 93:19   19 If you keep my commandments you too shall receive grace for grace.

Or in these words:

D&C 1:10   10 The Lord shall measure to every man according to the measure he has measured to his fellow man.

Salvation for all of us, then, can be seen in the parable only by combining the principles tied to each participant. For the man it was receiving help from one who otherwise might have been scorned (likened unto the reality that they yearned for a conquering Messiah and thereby rejected the suffering Messiah as prophesied in Isaiah 53).

The Savior's original intent seemed to urge us to act as the Samaritan, as a savior, and a minister to those in trouble regardless of social chasms. Salvation here came by ministering to others not just waiting to be ministered to. For the innkeeper, salvation came by accepting an assignment to minister to the needy and then agreeing to follow through. Over time this would include care in using furnished resources as well as a willingness to sacrifice personal resources in meeting the needs. This willingness would be sustained by faith in the promise of remuneration from he who symbolized the Savior as well as a relationship that allowed this trust or faith in his promised return. By combining the principles, we see "how we shall obtain eternal life"; how we shall love God and our neighbor with all our heart, and so forth. We see that the Atonement by which healing comes is a "participatory salvation" where the Savior, as he binds wounds, includes us in the saving process. This rehabilitation allows us to enter into an endowed partnership with the Master, which increases our capacity, tests our selflessness and charity, involves us in activities that perfect the very gifts with which he endows us, and thereby we are "perfected in him." He capacitates us by working *through* us not just *on* us as we then receive his grace by learning to give it. These perspectives of the Atonement serve, as clarified by Elder Bruce R. Hafen, to not only eliminate our weeds of sin but also to grow the divine flowers of our potential.[10] Clearly, by contrast, it is not just through fulfilling our administerial duties, like the careful Levite and priest who were prevented from ministering by the priorities of their position, but by responding to the needs of individual children of God. Joseph F. Smith emphasized this participatory salvation:

> *Jesus had not finished his work* when his body was slain, neither did he finish it after his resurrection from the dead; although he had accomplished the purpose for which he then came to the earth, he had not fulfilled all his work. And when will he? Not until he has redeemed and saved every son and daughter of our father Adam that have been or ever will be born upon this earth to the end of time, except the sons of perdition. That is his mission. *We will not finish our work until* we have saved ourselves, and then not until we shall have saved all depending upon us; for we are to become saviors upon Mount Zion, as well as Christ. We are called to this mission.[11]

John 14:12   12 He that believeth on me, the works that I do shall he do also; and greater works than these shall he do; because I go unto my Father.[12]

From the parable of the good Samaritan we can see that salvation, then, includes you and me acting in the stead of Christ as a joint-saviors (see D&C 103:9–10), the cleansing ordinances of the gospel, the participation of the Church, and the patient sacrificing management of those called to minister in their respective callings.

Were this the end of insights into how this parable helps us to apply the Atonement we would already be richly rewarded. The noble idea of self-sacrificing service is now elevated, if done in faithful partnership, to the level of a "sacrifice in similitude" (D&C 138:13) of the great model for all humankind. But looking more closely at the context gives birth to other pertinent questions. It is interesting that Luke is the only source of the parable. Matthew, Mark, and John don't include it. And then, Luke's use of this parable is out of order.[13] The chapter or section into which he imbeds this parable includes the calling and sending of the Seventy to the feast of the tabernacles, the return and report of the Seventy, and the incident with Mary and Martha. This period of time, the Feast of the Tabernacles, also includes the series of parables through Luke 15—John's telling of several healings and his lecture on the Good Shepherd.

Is it possible that the Savior's intent at the time of teaching the parable and his intent inspiring the gospel writers is different or perhaps enlarged beyond just an answer to a skeptical lawyer? Perhaps Luke was inspired in using the parable, with its original intent, to expand the message of the parable, thereby giving it even greater application and detail to a partici- patory salvation. If so, it is helpful to list the events and accompanying teachings, chaining them together in order to see the aggregate message otherwise missed in reading them separately. Of course, chapter breaks and versing were later additions, so care must be taken to find starting and stopping points in the narrative. Just as an example of what might be seen, let's note the listed items in Luke 10:1–42.

The chapter begins with the calling and subsequent sending of the Seventy. Then, without reference to time, Luke has them report their mis- sions immediately. This is followed by the parable of the good Samaritan, and then the story of Mary and Martha. It is noteworthy that this also takes place around the Feast of the Tabernacles as we shall see in examin- ing the traditions surrounding the feast.

Luke 10:1–42

1 After these things the Lord ap- pointed other seventy also, and sent them two and two before his face into every city and place, whither he him- self would come.
2 Therefore said he unto them, The harvest truly is great, but the labourers are few: pray ye therefore the Lord of the harvest, that he would send forth labourers into his harvest.
3 Go your ways: behold, I send you forth as lambs among wolves.
4 Carry neither purse, nor scrip, nor shoes: and salute no man by the way.

The feast is held in the fall to celebrate several things as its alter- nate names suggest: Feast of Lights and Feast of the In-gathering. It was the greatest and most joyful of all the feasts. Symbolically it was held in their seventh month and lasted thirteen days. The sacrifices offered were more numerous than at any other feast. They began by offering thirteen bullocks, each day offering an increment less until the seventh day, where-upon seven were offered. Each of the bullocks symbolized the great and last offering of the Savior of the world (see Moses 5:7).

Added together, 13, 12, 11, 10, 9, 8, and 7 total 70 bullocks,[14] the number of missionary administrators called by the Lord at the time this chapter of Luke was written. They were called to go forth as under-shep-herds or in the words of D&C 103:9–10, "saviors of men." Seventy is not only a number that is echoed in the Feast of Tabernacles but it is also sig-nificant because of ancient world tradition following the flood and scatter-ing of men across the face of the world. Genesis 10, often called the Table of Nations, enumerates the nations of the scattered posterity of Noah, total-ing seventy. It would be reasonable that the gathering would take place by those called the Seventy. The pattern of their calling in Luke seems to echo the process prescribed for delegation by modern experts in organizational behavior and applicable to the consideration of our original parable.

This pattern allows the leader to accomplish more than he could alone by enlisting help from his prospective disciples in whom he can thereby mentor growth. This could then apply instructively to the managing of the inn, or church, in the parable of the good Samaritan. In order to min-ister to the wounds of the man, Church leaders must learn the patterns of leadership modeled by the Savior so as to involve as many as possible in this participatory salvation. So, it seems, he positions this delegation pattern as a prelude to the parable to form a "leadership chapter." There are many texts on effective leadership and steps to take in delegating to subordinates. The following is an example that correlates well with Luke's account of the Savior's calling, sending, and reporting of the Seventy.

1. Impart *vision* of the call and the results expected: 2, 7–15.	**Calling, Delegating, Reporting** **5** And into whatsoever house ye enter, first say, Peace be to this house. **6** And if the son of peace be there, your peace shall rest upon it: if not, it shall turn to you again.
2. Define *resources*: 5–7.	**7** And in the same house remain, eating and drinking such things as they give: for the labourer is worthy of his hire. Go not from house to house. **8** And into whatsoever city ye enter, and they re-
3. Define *limitations*: 3.	ceive you, eat such things as are set before you: **9** And heal the sick that are therein, and say unto them, The kingdom of God is come nigh unto you.

4. Establish the level of *responsibility*: 3, 5, 6.1.

1. Go do assigned task

2. Go do . . . return for more

3. Go see needs—ask what to do, return

4. Go see needs—do, report immediately

5. Go see needs, do, report routinely

A good leader, when possible, works to raise the capacity for responsibility of the disciples.

5. Define the *rewards*: 16, 24 (see report of the seventy 10:17).

6. Set *reporting* time, frequency, and expectations 17–24.[15]

10 But into whatsoever city ye enter, and they receive you not, go your ways out into the streets of the same, and say,

11 Even the very dust of your city, which cleaveth on us, we do wipe off against you: notwithstanding be ye sure of this, that the kingdom of God is come nigh unto you.

12 But I say unto you, that it shall be more tolerable in that day for Sodom, than for that city.

16 He that heareth you heareth me; and he that despiseth you despiseth me; and he that despiseth me despiseth him that sent me.

17 And the seventy returned again with joy, saying, Lord, even the devils are subject unto us through thy name.

18 And he said unto them, I beheld Satan as lightning fall from heaven.

19 Behold, I give unto you power to tread on serpents and scorpions, and over all the power of the enemy: and nothing shall by any means hurt you.

20 Notwithstanding in this rejoice not, that the spirits are subject unto you; but rather rejoice, because your names are written in heaven.

21 In that hour Jesus rejoiced in spirit, and said, I thank thee, O Father, Lord of heaven and earth, that thou hast hid these things from the wise and prudent, and hast revealed them unto babes: even so, Father; for so it seemed good in thy sight.

22 All things are delivered to me of my Father: and no man knoweth who the Son is, but the Father; and who the Father is, but the Son, and he to whom the Son will reveal him.

23 And he turned him unto his disciples, and said privately, Blessed are the eyes which see the things that ye see:

24 For I tell you, that many prophets and kings have desired to see those things which ye see, and have not seen them; and to hear those things which ye hear, and have not heard them.

After hearing their report in verse 17 he helps them focus on the real significance of their calling: not just that they had powerful priesthood but that the faithful use of that power in the fulfilling of their calling had written their names in heaven.

Having addressed the real rewards of faithful service, Luke then joins the Savior in an apparent polemic discussion with a lawyer, one who could read Hebrew in addition to the spoken Aramaic of the time, so that he was schooled in the details of the law.

It was a time when scholarship was elevated over inspiration. Having already discussed the details of the parable and the Lord's intent in using it with the lawyer, let us wonder about Luke's contextualization. He places it as a sequel to leadership training in the kingdom. Could his use of it enlarge upon the Savior's message to the returning Seventy? The Levite and the priest were faithful in keeping themselves clean so that they could fulfill that assignment given them: to serve in the temple.[16] But the Savior's message wasn't about administration but about ministering to individual needs, not just system requirements. Could Luke have been pointing to the need to serve the one, not just the calling? He would have us be ministering administrators.

25 And, behold, a certain lawyer stood up, and tempted him, saying, Master, what shall I do to inherit eternal life?
26 He said unto him, What is written in the law? how readest thou?
27 And he answering said, Thou shalt love the Lord thy God with all thy heart, and with all thy soul, and with all thy strength, and with all thy mind; and thy neighbour as thyself.
28 And he said unto him, Thou hast answered right: this do, and thou shalt live.
29 But he, willing to justify himself, said unto Jesus, And who is my neighbour?
30 And Jesus answering said, A certain man went down from Jerusalem to Jericho, and fell among thieves, which stripped him of his raiment, and wounded him, and departed, leaving him half dead.

Ministering Administration
31 And by chance there came down a certain priest that way: and when he saw him, he passed by on the other side.
32 And likewise a Levite, when he was at the place, came and looked on him, and passed by on the other side.
33 But a certain Samaritan, as he journeyed, came where he was: and when he saw him, he had compassion on him,
34 And went to him, and bound up his wounds, pouring in oil and wine, and set him on his own beast, and brought him to an inn, and took care of him.
35 And on the morrow when he departed, he took out two pence, and gave them to the host, and said unto him, Take care of him; and whatsoever thou spendest more, when I come again, I will repay thee.

36 Which now of these three, thinkest thou, was neighbour unto him that fell among the thieves?

37 And he said, He that shewed mercy on him. Then said Jesus unto him, Go, and do thou likewise.

To emphasize this principle, the next section is the Mary-Martha experience beginning in verse 38. This would have also taken place during the Feast of the Tabernacles and could have occurred in the small huts that worshippers built adjacent to their homes and frequented during the feast. Martha would have thus been encumbered with serving outside of the kitchen/house.

Efficient or Effective

38 Now it came to pass, as they went, that he entered into a certain village: and a certain woman named Martha received him into her house.

39 And she had a sister called Mary, which also sat at Jesus' feet, and heard his word.

40 But Martha was cumbered about much serving, and came to him, and said, Lord, dost thou not care that my sister hath left me to serve alone? bid her therefore that she help me.

41 And Jesus answered and said unto her, Martha, Martha, thou art careful and troubled about many things:

42 But one thing is needful: and Mary hath chosen that good part, which shall not be taken away from her.

Many have written about this incident either defending Martha's decision to serve, or celebrating Mary's prioritization of personal contact over performance of duty. Both seem to have relevance in the Savior's patient teaching of his disciples. As one teacher put it, "When dealing with time, things, and systems one can be efficient. But, when dealing with people, one must be effective." These leadership choices accentuate again the need to prioritize people and life over systems and programs. Elder Maxwell distilled this principle from the Mary-Martha story:

> Life situations and leadership situations often present us with Mary versus Martha type choices in terms of how we spend our time and the priority we assign to the tasks on our "agenda" of action. Mary "heard his word," exploiting a unique, one-time opportunity to learn from the Master. Martha had no doubt served hundreds of meals before and would serve hundreds after Jesus' visit. With our associates, partners, and children in a fleeting mortality, do we tend to make Martha or Mary choices?[17]

And so his invitation to his disciples was one that offered both the synergy of participation engaged with him in his work and the direction or focus of that work.

Matthew 11:28–30

28 Come unto me, all ye that labour and are heavy laden, and I will give you rest.

29 Take my yoke upon you, and learn of me; for I am meek and lowly in heart: and ye shall find rest unto your souls.

30 For my yoke is easy, and my burden is light.

His "yoke is easy" may be misleading, but a closer look at the intent helps us see the focus. In Greek, the yoke is not easy but "pleasing" and "focused on people"[18] rather than systems or programs. This yoke principle helps us understand the works, faith, and grace synergy. A yoke ties two workers together, in this case Christ, whose yoke it is, and us. But a yoke is only effective if the two linked parties pull together, matching each other's timing and pull strength. Elder Packer shared the importance of the principle by telling of watching two small but coordinating oxen out-pull two larger but more independent oxen. As we engage in or focus on the Savior's saving work, with faith that he will then help with our work, he matches our strength and timing. In so doing, he also capacitates us by making "weak things become strong." So our faith matched by our works allows him, through his grace, by working through us to bless others, to in-turn perfect us. This is undoubtedly the process to which the ancient Apostle Peter referred as he closed his mortal ministry:

2 Peter 3:18

18 But *grow in grace*, and in the knowledge of our Lord and Saviour Jesus Christ. To him be glory both now and for ever. Amen.

In summary, then, Luke has given us a teaching sequence that includes the parable of the good Samaritan, placing the Master in the role of the perfect leader about which President Kimball commented extensively:

His innate brilliance would have permitted him to put on a dazzling display, but that would have left his followers far behind. . . . His was not a long-distance leadership.

Jesus trusts his followers enough to share his work with them so that they can grow. . . . If we brush other people aside in order to see a task done more quickly and effectively, the task may get done all right, but without the growth and development in followers. . . .

Jesus was not afraid to make demands of those he led. . . . Jesus let
people know that he believed in them and in their possibilities, and thus
he was free to help them stretch their souls in fresh achievement. . . .

We must remember that those mortals we meet in parking lots, offices,
elevators, and elsewhere are that portion of mankind God has given us to
love and to serve. . . . If our sample of humanity seems unglamorous or so
very small, we need to remember . . . [Jesus] reminded us that greatness is
not always a matter of size or scale, but of the quality of one's life.

The tyranny of trivia consists of its driving out the people and
moments that really matter. Minutia holds momentous things hostage. . . .
Wise time management is really the wise management of ourselves.[19]

Furthermore the Feast of the Tabernacles is the occasion of several
parables that seem to carry this ministering theme of the parable of the
good Samaritan. Luke seems to be preparing a future leadership of the
Meridian Church by continuing in chapter fifteen with the three parables
of ministering to those lost. In this context it would seem to instruct us in
our church leadership approach toward those lost who, like lambs, simply
got lost; or like the coin, were lost due to the carelessness of a leader; or like
the prodigal whose straying was willful and rebellious. Where the parable
of the good Samaritan modeled the means of personal salvation through
consecrated service, these parables instruct in the particulars of meeting the
differing circumstances to be encountered. Ministering is people focused;
people are different, and therefore the manner of ministering is different.
Home and visiting teaching can be administered as a program but can
only be lived as individual ministers to individual and different people.

These parables and teachings merge to invite us to a participatory
salvation that would transform not only those that we lead but also us as
ministering leaders through the enabling power of the great Atonement.
This is portrayed as an ongoing process whereby God capacitates us as he
changes us by working through us, to the end that we might be perfect *in*
Christ (see Moroni 10:32).

Notes

1. See John Welch, "The Good Samaritan: A Type and Shadow of the
Plan of Salvation," *BYU Studies,* vol. 38, no. 2, 1999, 51–115 for
references to the writings of the ancients on the allegorization of
the parable. Similar interpretative variations of the parable are also
done independently by Hugh Nibley, Brent Farley, Stephen Robin-
son, Lisle Brown, and Jill Major as listed by John Welch.

2. Ibid., 55, 73.

3. McConkie, *Doctrinal New Testament Commentary*, 2:230

4. Harold B. Lee, *Stand Ye in Holy Places* (Salt Lake City: Deseret Book, 1974), 51–52.

5. *Encyclopedia of Mormonism*, ed. by Daniel H. Ludlow (New York: Macmillan, 1992), 810.

6. Joseph Fielding McConkie and Robert L. Millet, *Doctrinal Commentary on the Book of Mormon* (Salt Lake City: Bookcraft, 1991), 3:315.

7. *Encyclopedia of Mormonism*, 810.

8. James E. Talmage, *Jesus the Christ: A Study of the Messiah and His Mission According to Holy Scriptures Both Ancient and Modern* (Salt Lake City: The Church of Jesus Christ of Latter-day Saints, 1981), 627.

9. Young Adult CES Broadcast, Boyd K. Packer, 7 Nov. 1993.

10. Elder Bruce C. Hafen, "The Atonement: All for All," in Conference Report, May 2004, 97; "We need grace both to overcome sinful weeds and to grow divine flowers."

11. Joseph F. Smith, *Gospel Doctrine*, 5th ed. (Salt Lake City: Deseret Book, 1939), 442; emphasis added.

12. These are the Savior's instructions to his Apostles in the upper room just before delivering himself up to Gethsemane. The "greater work" here surely refers to the scope of the work because he had to go to his Father.

13. See Alfred Eidersheim, *The Life and Times of Jesus the Messiah*, 144; see also Holzapfel, Huntsman, Wayment, *Jesus Christ and the World of the New Testament*, 116.

14. Alfred Eidersheim, *The Temple*, 276–77.

15. See Stephen R. Covey, *The 7 Habits of Highly Effective People* (New York: Simon & Schuster, 1989), 171–79.

16. The law of Moses dictated that to be soiled with the blood of another or to touch the body of a dead person renders one ritually unclean. (See Leviticus 21:10; Numbers 19:11–16; 35:32–33; Deuteronomy 22:8.) The risks to these men of the temple included long involvement in ritual cleansing and possible death of the man, making it necessary to legally be absolved of the guilt of his death. All this and more yield an administrative expediency to pass by the other side so as to be left clean and capable of fulfilling their primary duties of the priesthood.

17. Neal A. Maxwell, *"For the Power Is in Them . . .": Mormon Musings* (Salt Lake City: Deseret Book, 1970), 11.

18. LDS Collector's Reference Library: Strong's Dictionary Number 5543-chrestos {khrase-tos} Greek: adjective Possible Definitions: (1) fit, fit for use, useful; virtuous, good, and (2) manageable, i.e. mild, pleasant, of things: more pleasant, of people, kind, benevolent.

19. Spencer W. Kimball, "Jesus: The Perfect Leader," *Ensign*, Aug. 1979, 5–7.

The Rich Man and Lazarus

Conditions in the World to Come

by Andrew C. Skinner

How many times have we heard something like "Life isn't fair" or "There is no justice in the world"? In the parable of the rich man and Lazarus, Jesus teaches us that while such sentiments may be true in this life, there is a day coming when all injustice will be overturned and all the unfairness that accompanies mortality will be made up to those who have sought to live uprightly. Justice will become the friend of those who have become the friend of God "and him that seeketh so to do" (D&C 46:9). On the last night of his mortal life, Jesus declared that in this present world his disciples would have tribulations, but they were still to be of good cheer because he had overcome the world and so would they (see John 16:33). The conditions that exist in the world to come are not controlled by the wealthy or the powerful, as the world measures these things, but by a God who, possessing all power and all knowledge, is perfectly just and perfectly merciful. Such are the defining messages of the parable of the rich man and Lazarus.

Setting

As the time of his suffering and Atonement approached inexorably, Jesus increased the pace of his teaching and the circle of his influence. Consequently, the number of events reported in the Gospels for the third year of his public ministry is three times the number recorded for the first year. The giving of the parable of the rich man and Lazarus came toward the end of that monumental third year. Already past were the critical experiences on the Mount of Transfiguration, when the keys of the kingdom were delivered to the Apostles, and they saw in vision the transfiguration of the earth. We know that the Mount of Transfiguration events happened in the fall season, around the Feast of Tabernacles, five or six months before the greatest Passover in the history of the world unfolded—when Jesus himself became the Passover offering. During that intervening half year, Jesus embarked on even more intense teaching tours through Judea and Perea. Therefore we are reasonably sure Jesus taught the parable in question sometime during his Perean ministry. And, in fact, most Gospel harmonies put the location of the delivery of the parable of the rich man and Lazarus in the region of Perea.[1]

This is significant for it helps us to see more readily the connection between the only parable mentioning the name of a specific individual, Lazarus, and an actual event wherein a man also named Lazarus was raised from the dead by Jesus (see John 11:1–44). The setting of the latter episode is well known. Jesus was in Perea when news arrived that his beloved friend, Lazarus, brother of Martha and Mary, was sick. There is reason to believe that Jesus was told of the gravity of the illness because he specifically stated:

John 11:4   4 This sickness is not unto death, but for the glory of God, that the Son of God might be glorified thereby.

One has the sense that it was this news and this news only that got Jesus to leave Perea at that time and head back to Judea, where the Jewish leaders sought to kill him. Elder James E. Talmage noted, "The duration of this sojourn in Perea is nowhere recorded in our scriptures. . . . From this retreat of comparative quiet, Jesus returned to Judea in response to an earnest appeal from some whom he loved. He left the Bethany of Perea for the Judean Bethany, where dwelt Martha and Mary."[2]

Of course, the hinge on which the rest of the story pivots is Jesus' waiting two whole days, "still in the same place where he was," before going to the aid of Lazarus (John 11:6). There was purpose in this waiting. It allowed Lazarus to die, to experience the spirit world, and it set up the situation whereby Jesus' prophecy, mentioned above (see John 11:4), was fulfilled. But our interest at this juncture centers on what went on in Perea during those two days he remained there. We do not know, but is it possible that Jesus took the occasion to recount a parable that used the circumstance of his friend's death to teach doctrines central to the plan of salvation? We think so. We know that Jesus was in Perea when he learned of Lazarus's illness, when Lazarus died, and when Jesus recounted the parable of Lazarus's experience after Lazarus died. We know that the death of Lazarus is central to both the parable and the episode involving Lazarus's resuscitation. We know that both the parable and the episode contain the unusual name Lazarus. We know that in both the parable and the episode, Lazarus is a righteous man. And we know that central to both parable and episode is the power of Jesus' Atonement. One is a description of how acceptance of the Atonement affects our standing in the next world. The other is a real-life foreshadowing of the ultimate power of the Atonement—coming back to life through the Resurrection.

Elements of the Parable

Stories contrasting the positions of two men in the world to come, based on their righteousness and repentance (or lack of it) in this life, are known from the period roughly contemporaneous with Jesus' mortal life.[3] It is possible, perhaps even likely, that he heard such stories while growing up and incorporated them into his vast repertoire of teaching skills and techniques. Certainly the parable of the rich man and Lazarus contains some of the specific elements of the other versions found in the rabbinic and intertestamental bodies of literature. But the fact that Jesus weaves together all of the disparate elements of different parables into one story in a way that brings us back squarely to the warning voices of the prophets and ends with an unmistakable reference to the reality of the Resurrection make Jesus' story truly powerful and unique.

The parable of the rich man and Lazarus has different subthemes: the importance of using wealth properly; the danger of worldliness; selfishness; and the importance of listening to the warning voices of the prophets—both living and dead. But its ultimate message and greatest contribution is the flood of light it adds to our understanding of the state of souls between death and the Resurrection.[4]

The parable opens by contrasting an unnamed man of significant wealth with the protagonist, the lowliest of beggars, named Lazarus. This is the Greek form of the Hebrew name Eliezar, shortened in Palestinian Jewish usage to Lazar. Ironically, the name means literally "the one whom God helps."[5] Thus, right from the beginning, the parable points us to

God's power and Atonement through the very name of the righteous hero in the story. In a nice contrast of his own, Elder Talmage notes that "the afflicted beggar is honored with a name; the other is designated simply as 'a certain rich man.' "[6] This, in turn, recalls Jehovah's ancient promise: "Them that honour me I will honour, and they that despise me shall be lightly esteemed" (1 Samuel 2:30). The rich man was not honored with a name.

That the rich man wore purple (see Luke 16:19) suggests royalty. Jesus may have even included this detail to foreshadow his endurance of cruel mockery at the hands of Roman soldiers while standing trial before Pilate (see Mark 15:16–18). Lazarus is so poor that he sat at the rich man's gate and longed to eat the crumbs from the rich man's table. His circumstance is so pathetic that dogs came and licked his sores (see Luke 16:21).

The significance of this added detail would not have been lost on Jesus' audience, for the rabbis taught, "There are those whose life is no life: he who depends on the table of another [for food] . . . and he whose body is burdened with sufferings."[7] In addition, dogs were viewed as unclean animals, and they here reflect the depth of the poor man's misery.[8] Jesus undoubtedly knew that his listeners were familiar with this societal norm. He wanted his listeners to understand the profundity of the contrast he was drawing between the two characters in the story. According to their own Jewish standards, Lazarus had less than nothing—no life! How great a reversal then would be seen in the fortunes of the two men when Jesus described their respective conditions after they died.

Sure enough, when Lazarus died he was carried by angels to Abraham's bosom (see Luke 16:22). This was a Jewish idiom most often used in rabbinic sources for righteous martyrs. Considering the towering position of Abraham in Israelite religion, and the high regard in which he was held by the Jews of Jesus' day (see John 8:53; James 2:23), this would have been high praise indeed for Lazarus. Elder McConkie notes that Abraham's bosom is "Paradise, the temporary abode of righteous Abraham as he awaited the day of his resurrection; all righteous disembodied spirits are received into this spirit realm where they rest from the turmoils and physical toils of mortality, but continue their labors as intelligent, sentient souls as they await their resurrection."[9]

Jesus' reference to the escort provided to Lazarus by angels also reflects Jewish religious and literary ideas current in that day, ideas with which Jesus' listeners would have been familiar. As a general rule, it was believed that the soul of the departed was taken by the angel of death. Those who were exceptionally worthy were "escorted by Gabriel and Michael."[10] At death there could be no deception about, or manipulation of, one's true standing before God. As the pseudepigraphical work, Testament of Asher, declares, "For the latter ends of man do show their righteousness (or unrighteousness), when they meet the angels of the Lord and of Satan. For when the soul departs troubled, it is tormented by the evil spirit which also it served in lusts and evil works. But, if he is peaceful with joy he meeteth the angel of peace, and he leadeth him into eternal life."[11]

Accordingly, the rich man, who did not heed the prophets in mortality, found himself in hell—a place separate and apart from Lazarus's abode. Being in torment, he lifted up his eyes and saw both Abraham and Lazarus afar off (see Luke 16:23). It has been suggested that the rich man in the parable was understood to be a Sadducee. As such, the fact that in mortality he did not believe in a conscious afterlife, but in death became fully aware of his error, made his torment all the greater. He now knew of the defining and physically demarcating division in the afterlife between the righteous and the wicked.

The word in the Greek text of this passage translated as *hell* is Hades, literally the place of departed spirits opposite Abraham's bosom. The lesson was already becoming clear to Jesus' listeners. In mortality, riches without righteousness mean nothing in God's view. On the other hand, total, abject, consuming poverty, if endured in righteousness, means everything to God and will be rewarded and recompensed.

The Parable and the Atonement

In this modern dispensation, the Lord taught plainly the definitive and powerful lessons to be derived from the parable of the rich man and Lazarus, which his contemporary audience should have grasped. In language reminiscent of the parable, Jesus declared the following through the Prophet Joseph Smith:

D&C 56:16–19

16 Wo unto you rich men, that will not give your substance to the poor, for your riches will canker your souls; and this shall be your lamentation in the day of visitation, and of judgment, and of indignation: The harvest is past, the summer is ended, and my soul is not saved!

17 Wo unto you poor men, whose hearts are

not broken, whose spirits are not contrite, and
whose bellies are not satisfied, and whose hands
are not stayed from laying hold upon other
men's goods, whose eyes are full of greediness,
and who will not labor with your own hands!

18 But blessed are the poor who are pure in
heart, whose hearts are broken, and whose spirits are contrite, for they shall see the kingdom
of God coming in power and great glory unto
their deliverance; for the fatness of the earth
shall be theirs.

19 For behold, the Lord shall come, and his
recompense shall be with him, and he shall
reward every man, and the poor shall rejoice.

The golden thread running through this passage is not the surface
doctrine, which asks the rich to give to the poor and asks the poor to be
grateful for what is given and not covet. This is important and obvious.
Rather the deeper, more profound and foundational doctrine underlying
the Savior's words is the injunction to cultivate a broken heart and a contrite spirit, and these two requirements both take us back to, and are at
the heart of, the Atonement of Jesus Christ. When the resurrected Jesus
manifested himself to those living in the New World, he forever changed
the nature of the ancient sacrifices, which had stood as symbols, types,
and shadows of the Atonement for thousands of years.

3 Nephi 9:19–20

19 And ye shall offer up unto me no more the
shedding of blood; yea, your sacrifices and your
burnt offerings shall be done away, for I will accept
none of your sacrifices and your burnt offerings.

20 And ye shall offer for a sacrifice unto me a
broken heart and a contrite spirit.

A broken heart and a contrite spirit are a perfect likeness of Jesus'
atoning experience, and by asking all disciples to cultivate these characteristics, he is really bidding us to comprehend the nature of his atoning
experience. The word *contrite* comes directly from a Latin root meaning
"to grind." To be contrite is to be "crushed in spirit."[12] In Gethsemane,
Jesus' spirit was crushed by the weight of the sins and sorrows of the world
(remember he said he felt "very heavy," or weighed down; Mark 14:33).
In Gethsemane, Jesus was ground and crushed like an olive (*Gethsemane*

literally means "oil press"). And on Golgotha's cross, "Jesus died of a *broken heart*," the consequence of suffering for infinite sin and sorrow.[13]

Therefore, to cultivate a broken heart and a contrite spirit is to experience what Jesus experienced and to know personally the effect the Atonement had on Jesus. To offer up a broken heart and a contrite spirit is to give to the poor and needy willingly, to be grateful for gifts given to us, to eschew greed and selfishness, to vanquish pride, to repent, to cultivate meekness (poise in the face of provocation), and to patiently submit to all things that the Father sees fit to inflict upon us. It is to suffer anguish, even godly sorrow, for our own sins as well as feel pain for the sorrows of others. In short, to cultivate a broken heart and a contrite spirit is to do everything the rich man did not do, and to be everything that Lazarus was.

One of the most impressive ways that the power of the Atonement and redemption of Jesus Christ is illustrated in the parable comes about through the dialogue Jesus creates between the rich man and Father Abraham. The rich man begs for relief from his tormenting circumstances. But Abraham responds with pure doctrine. First, he teaches that in the world to come, unlike this mortal sphere, perfect justice and perfect fairness hold sway. Righteousness, including both actions and desires (see D&C 137:9), not only count in the equation, they *are* the equation when it comes to determining status in the eternities. Without righteous behavior, worldly success (or success as the world measures it) does not bring eternal life. As Abraham says to the rich man,

Luke 16:25	25 Son, remember that thou in thy lifetime receivest thy good things, and likewise Lazarus evil things: but now he is comforted, and thou art tormented.

This statement is very good news to those whose lot in life has been hard, filled with trials, tribulations, tragedies, sorrows, and suffering, but who have tried to live as God has wanted them to, and who have determined to be loyal to God through all hazards. It is good news because it constitutes a promise that all of mortality's unfairness and injustice will be overturned and made up to the righteous, as in the case of Lazarus. Of course, Abraham's (Jesus') response does not imply that the righteous will (or more importantly, desire to) cheer at the suffering of the wicked. Rather, it confirms to all true disciples that there is a time coming when, as Revelation says,

Revelation 21:4   4 God shall wipe away all tears from their eyes; and there shall be no more death, neither sorrow, nor crying, neither shall there be any more pain: for the former things are passed away.

All aspects of this mighty reversal are accomplished through the Atonement, the power of the redemption and resurrection that is in Jesus Christ. Through the Atonement, faithful disciples of the Savior receive the best of both worlds, so to speak. They receive the blessings of the law of mercy, which ensures they *do not* get what they deserve because the demands of justice are satisfied, broken laws are answered, and required payment for sin is provided (see Alma 42:14–15). Thus, through the Atonement and redemption offered by Jesus Christ, mercy becomes their friend (see Alma 42:23). Yet, they also receive the blessings of the law of justice, which ensures that they *do* get what they deserve in terms of recompensing them for all of life's injustices. Therefore, through the Atonement and redemption offered by Jesus Christ, justice too becomes their friend:

Alma 41:13–14   13 The meaning of the word restoration is to bring back again evil for evil, or carnal for carnal, or devilish for devilish—good for that which is good; righteous for that which is righteous; just for that which is just; merciful for that which is merciful.
14 Therefore, my son, see that you are merciful unto your brethren; deal justly, judge righteously, and do good continually; and if ye do all these things then shall ye receive your reward; yea, ye shall have mercy restored unto you again; ye shall have justice restored unto you again; ye shall have a righteous judgment restored unto you again; and ye shall have good rewarded unto you again.

The parable of the rich man and Lazarus is a marvelous illustration of that foundational principle. There is a difference between mere payment for sin and complete redemption from the effects of sin and suffering. The Atonement accomplishes both payment and complete restoration to a pristine spiritual condition that puts us in a right relationship with Deity, which is the doctrine of justification (see Galatians 2:16; D&C 45:3–5).

Conditions in the Spirit World

The second part of Abraham's response (which is really Jesus' doctrinal declaration) to the rich man's plea for relief by sending Lazarus with cool, refreshing water teaches us about the actual conditions that exist in the spirit world. This doctrine had not been taught previously in Jesus' ministry with such clarity. Even if Lazarus were inclined to leave his newly acquired paradisiacal condition to enter the environment of hell where the rich man languished, he could not. Says Abraham in the parable,

Luke 16:26

26 And beside all this, between us and you there is a great gulf fixed: so that they which would pass from hence to you cannot; neither can they pass to us, that would come from thence.

The concept of a great gulf in the world of spirits is attested elsewhere in the Jewish literature of the intertestamental period. But our most helpful and illuminating texts on the subject come from the Book of Mormon.

The Prophet Nephi saw this great gulf of which Jesus spoke through the dialogue he put into the mouth of Abraham in the parable. Said Nephi:

1 Nephi 15:28–30

28 And I said unto them that it was an awful gulf, which separated the wicked from the tree of life, and also from the saints of God.

29 And I said unto them that it was a representation of that awful hell, which the angel said unto me was prepared for the wicked.

30 And I said unto them that our father also saw that the justice of God did also divide the wicked from the righteous; and the brightness thereof was like unto the brightness of a flaming fire, which ascendeth up unto God forever and ever, and hath no end.

The Prophet Alma also described in complete detail the great gulf of Jesus' parable many years before the parable was uttered. He said,

Alma 40:11–14

11 Now, concerning the state of the soul

between death and the resurrection—Behold,
it has been made known unto me by an angel,
that the spirits of all men, as soon as they are
departed from this mortal body, yea, the spirits
of all men, whether they be good or evil, are
taken home to that God who gave them life.
12 And then shall it come to pass, that the spirits of those who are righteous are received into
a state of happiness, which is called paradise, a
state of rest, a state of peace, where they shall
rest from all their troubles and from all care,
and sorrow.
13 And then shall it come to pass, that the spirits of the wicked, yea, who are evil—for behold,
they have no part nor portion of the Spirit of the
Lord; for behold, they chose evil works rather
than good; therefore the spirit of the devil did
enter into them, and take possession of their
house—and these shall be cast out into outer
darkness; there shall be weeping, and wailing,
and gnashing of teeth, and this because of their
own iniquity, being led captive by the will of
the devil.
14 Now this is the state of the souls of the
wicked, yea, in darkness, and a state of awful,
fearful looking for the fiery indignation of the
wrath of God upon them; thus they remain in
this state, as well as the righteous in paradise,
until the time of their resurrection.

Elder Bruce R. McConkie's summary statement on this point is very
helpful.

There was no intermingling by the spirits in paradise and hell until
after Christ bridged the "great gulf" between these two spirit abodes
(Alma 40:11–14). This he did while his body lay in the tomb of Joseph
of Arimathea and his own disembodied spirit continued to minister
to men in their spirit prison (1 Peter 3:18–21; 4:6; Joseph F. Smith,
Gospel Doctrine, 5th ed., pp. 472–476). "Until that day" the prison-
ers remained bound and the gospel was not preached to them (Moses
7:37–39). The hope of salvation for the dead was yet to come.

But now, since our Lord has proclaimed "liberty to the captives, and the opening of the prison to them that are bound" (Isa. 61:1), the gospel is preached in all parts of the spirit world, repentance is granted to those who seek it, vicarious ordinances are administered in earthly temples, and there is a hope of salvation for the spirits of those men who would have received the gospel with all their hearts in this life had the opportunity come to them (*Teachings*, p. 107). At this time, as Joseph Smith explained it, "Hades, sheol, paradise, spirits in prison, are all one: it is a world of spirits" (*Teachings*, p. 310).[14]

Clearly, the atoning mission of our Lord included his disembodied visit to the world of spirits, and his organization of missionary forces to liberate the spirits in captivity was a fulfillment of his own promise uttered as the premortal Jehovah and then repeated in the Nazareth synagogue (see Isaiah 61:1; Luke 4:18). Much has been revealed about this stunning aspect of his redemptive ministry (see D&C 138). It is part of the Atonement; it delivered the captive spirits from bondage and from hell.

D&C 138:50

50 For the dead had looked upon the long absence of their spirits from their bodies as a bondage.

But there is also another way in which the Atonement of Jesus Christ provides relief and release to the rich man of the parable, and all like him, living in spirit prison or hell. This is the Resurrection. The Book of Mormon prophet Jacob testified of this fact.

2 Nephi 9:6, 8–10

6 For as death hath passed upon all men, to fulfil the merciful plan of the great Creator, there must needs be a power of resurrection, and the resurrection must needs come unto man by reason of the Fall; and the Fall came by reason of transgression; and because man became fallen they were cut off from the presence of the Lord. . . .

8 O the wisdom of God, his mercy and grace! For behold, if the flesh should rise no more our spirits must become subject to that angel who fell from before the presence of the Eternal God, and became the devil, to rise no more.

9 And our spirits must have become like unto him, and we become devils, angels to a devil, to be shut out from the presence of our God, and

> to remain with the father of lies, in misery, like unto himself; yea, to that being who beguiled our first parents, who transformeth himself nigh unto an angel of light, and stirreth up the children of men unto secret combinations of murder and all manner of secret works of darkness.
>
> **10** O how great the goodness of our God, who prepareth a way for our escape from the grasp of this awful monster; yea, that monster, death and hell, which I call the death of the body, and also the death of the spirit.

In other words, resurrection is itself redemption! It rescues all (except sons of perdition) from what would be an endless spiritual degeneration in the clutches of Satan and his followers. It is a redemptive gift given to all human beings (see Alma 11:41).

A Concluding Warning

Jesus concluded his parable about the rich man and Lazarus by teaching his listeners the absolute necessity of listening to prophetic voices while in mortality. God chooses his own special messengers to raise the warning signal and keep his children safe from spiritual dangers. There is something of an insinuation on the part of the rich man that "Moses and the prophets" (meaning both the scriptures and living prophets) were not an adequate and fair warning, and he requested the opportunity to provide a better warning to his five brothers, "lest they also come into this place of torment" (Luke 16:28).

Such reasoning strikes one as typical rationalization—the impulse to blame one's circumstances on other people or occurrences. Hence, in the parable we see Jesus demonstrate his superior knowledge of the human psyche, as he countered false arguments with divine understanding. Those who refuse to heed scriptural and prophetic counsel will not heed unmistakable miracles or even resurrected beings. As the Lord said in this dispensation, "Faith [to heed divine counsel] cometh not by signs, but signs follow those that believe" (D&C 63:9). Thus, "If they hear not Moses and the prophets, neither will they be persuaded, though one rose from the dead" (Luke 16:31).

As Elder Talmage indicates, this teaching was "an instructive rebuke for the derision and scorn with which they [Jesus' audience] had received the Lord's warning concerning the dangers attending servitude to Mammon."[17] In our day the lesson seems broader and deeper, though perhaps a bit more subtle. We must not allow *anything*, wealth, position, or learning, to interfere with our ability to take divine counsel. We must constantly cultivate humility. The Book of Mormon, perhaps the greatest commentary as a whole on the parable of the rich man and Lazarus, warns in stern terms that the two groups of people who stand in greatest jeopardy of being despised—yes, despised—by the Lord are the proud who are rich (no surprise) and the proud who are learned.

2 Nephi 9:42   42 And whoso knocketh, to him will he open; and the wise, and the learned, and they that are rich, who are puffed up because of their learning, and their wisdom, and their riches—yea, they are they whom he despiseth; and save they shall cast these things away, and consider themselves fools before God, and come down in the depths of humility, he will not open unto them.

Perhaps that is *the* meaning and application of the parable of the rich man and Lazarus for the twenty-first century.

As both a parable of redemption, and a parable speaking to the critical issues of our day, the parable of the rich man and Lazarus stands supreme. On almost all points and levels, it directs our attention to the greatest dangers of mortality and the only real remedy—the power of the Atonement of Jesus Christ. This is not by accident or coincidence since the most important event in time and all eternity is the Atonement of Jesus Christ, and his desire for each of us is that we gain a personal witness of his divine Sonship and messianic position.

For *all* those who have experienced life's unfairness (betrayal, crippling illness, singleness, loneliness, poverty, and so forth), a kind of unfairness made more stark and acute by one's whole-hearted attempt to please God, the parable of the rich man and Lazarus was given. Too often, I fear, we focus on the punishment of the rich man when we might more profitably contemplate the blessedness of Lazarus. Perhaps we ought to pray more consistently for the ability to endure faithfully in mortality until the day of recompense and redemption arrives. For make no mistake, it will arrive!

Notes

1. See, for example, Thomas M. Mumford, *Horizontal Harmony of the Four Gospels in Parallel Columns* (Salt Lake City: Deseret Book, 1976), x; or Bible Dictionary, "harmony of the Gospels," 691.
2. Talmage, *Jesus the Christ*, 490.
3. Note, for example, the two recounted in Samuel Tobias Lachs, *A Rabbinic Commentary on the New Testament* (Hoboken, NJ: KTAV Publishing House, 1987), 313–14. These are taken from the Jerusalem Talmud and from the Midrashic Collection.
4. McConkie, *Doctrinal New Testament Commentary*, 1:519.
5. Lachs, *Rabbinic Commentary on the New Testament*, 314.
6. Talmage, *Jesus the Christ*, 466.
7. Babylonian Talmud, Baba Bez. 32b; as quoted in Lachs, *Rabbinic Commentary on the New Testament*, 314.
8. *The Interpreter's Bible* (Nashville: Abingdon, 1978), 8:291.
9. McConkie, *Doctrinal New Testament Commentary*, 1:521.
10. Lachs, *Rabbinic Commentary on the New Testament*, 314.
11. The Testament of Asher 6:4–6; as quoted in R. H. Charles, "The Testament of the Twelve Patriarchs," *The Apocrypha and Pseudepigrapha of the Old Testament in English* (Oxford: Clarendon Press, 1977), 2:345.
12. *Webster's New World Dictionary of the American Language*, "contrite," 321.
13. Talmage, *Jesus the Christ*, 669; emphasis added.
14. McConkie, *Doctrinal New Testament Commentary*, 1:521–22.

INDEX

A B O U T   T H E
A U T H O R S

C. ROBERT LINE: Brother Line played on the men's basketball team at Brigham Young University (BYU) and served a mission in the Ecuador Quito Mission. He received his bachelor's and master's degrees from BYU and later a doctorate in the sociology of religion from Purdue University. He is a full-time instructor at the Institute of Religion adjacent to the University of Utah. In addition to being the editor-in-chief of *Century Magazine,* he teaches part-time in the religion department at BYU and for a variety of BYU continuing education programs, including EFY and Education Week. Brother Line has authored various articles and essays and has given symposia presentations on LDS doctrine, history, and religious instruction.

Brother Line and his wife, Tami, are the parents of five children.

RONALD E. BARTHOLOMEW: Brother Bartholomew served a mission to Pusan, Korea, and then received his bachelor's and master's degrees from BYU and a doctorate in the sociology of education from the University of Buckingham in London, England. He is now an instructor at the Institute adjacent to Utah Valley State College in Orem. He also teaches part-time in the religion department at BYU and for a variety of BYU continuing education programs, including EFY, Best of EFY, and Education Week. He also currently serves as a bishop.

Brother Bartholomew and his wife, Kristen, are the parents of seven children.

R. SCOTT BURTON: Brother Burton is originally from Kokomo, Indiana. After serving a mission in the Massachusetts Boston Mission, he attended BYU, where he received his bachelor's degree in anthropology/archaeology. Upon leaving BYU, he attended the University of Michigan, where he received a master's in Near Eastern studies. He has published several chapters in Old Testament commentaries and is currently a coordinator for the Church Educational System in Columbus, Ohio.

Brother Burton and his wife, Estelle, are the parents of four children.

ROBERT ENGLAND LEE: Originally from Pocatello, Idaho, Brother Lee has been employed by the LDS Church Educational System for twenty-nine years and is currently a member of the faculty of the Salt Lake University Institute of Religion. He has served as a bishop and mission president and has a doctorate in education from BYU.

Brother Lee and his wife, Peggy, are the parents of eight and grandparents of fifteen.

CRAIG FROGLEY: Brother Frogley has formally taught the gospel for thirty-one years. He served a mission to France and then obtained his bachelor's degree from BYU and his doctorate of chiropractic from Palmer College. Though teaching professionally, he has maintained an active chiropractic practice for thirty-two years. He received a master's in leadership from the Covey Leadership Institute. He serves on the Board of Trustees for the Joseph Smith Sr. and Lucy Mack Smith Foundation. He is the author of a multimedia teaching CD and numerous articles.

Brother Frogley and wife, Janet, are the parents of eight children and grandparents of seven. They reside in Sandy, Utah.

ANDREW C. SKINNER: Brother Skinner served a mission to California before receiving a bachelor's degree in history from the University of Colorado, a master of arts in Hebrew Bible–Judaic Studies from the Iliff School of Theology, a master of theology in Biblical Hebrew from Harvard University, and a doctorate in European and Near Eastern history from the University of Denver. He has served as the Dean of Religious Education at BYU and now serves as Executive Director of the Neal A. Maxwell Institute for Religious Scholarship at BYU. He is also a professor of ancient scripture at BYU.

Brother Skinner and his wife, Janet, are the parents of six children.